2024

Berufliches Gymnasium
Original-Prüfungsaufgaben mit Lösungen

Baden-Württemberg

Englisch

STARK

© 2023 Stark Verlag GmbH
20. neu bearbeitete und ergänzte Auflage
www.stark-verlag.de

Das Werk und alle seine Bestandteile sind urheberrechtlich geschützt. Jede vollständige oder teilweise Vervielfältigung, Verbreitung und Veröffentlichung bedarf der ausdrücklichen Genehmigung des Verlages. Dies gilt insbesondere für Vervielfältigungen, Mikroverfilmungen sowie die Speicherung und Verarbeitung in elektronischen Systemen.

Inhaltsverzeichnis

Vorwort
Hinweise zu den digitalen Zusätzen

Hinweise und Tipps zur Abiturprüfung

1 Struktur der schriftlichen Abiturprüfung I
2 Gewichtung der einzelnen Prüfungsteile III
3 Praxistipps und sprachliche Hilfen zu den Aufgaben IV

Übungsaufgaben zum Hörverstehen

Übungsaufgabe 1: *Renting a house or apartment* 1
Übungsaufgabe 2: *Floodings in the UK* 5
Übungsaufgabe 3: *Happiness by design* 10
Übungsaufgabe 4: *Journalism and its audiences* 14
Übungsaufgabe 5: *Protecting the climate* 18
Übungsaufgabe 6: *Robotics* 21
Übungsaufgabe 7: *Brooklyn film school located in working film lot* 25
Übungsaufgabe 8: *Most adolescents do not exercise enough to stay healthy* 29

Übungsaufgaben zum Lesen und Schreiben

Übungsaufgabe 1: *Jess Phillips, "Women suffer guilt, abuse and disapproval. no wonder Jacinda Ardern is knackered"* 33
Übungsaufgabe 2: *Our 21st-century segregation: we're still divided by race* 46
Übungsaufgabe 3: *Why media commentary is so crucial when opinions displace facts* 55
Übungsaufgabe 4: *UNHCR and IOM call for a truly common and principled approach to European migration and asylum policies* 65

Offizielle Musterprüfung

Teil I: Hörverstehen	MP-1
Teil II: Lesen und Schreiben (Aufgabenset 1)	MP-5
Teil II: Lesen und Schreiben (Aufgabenset 2)	MP-8
Teil III: Kommunikationsprüfung	MP-11
Lösungen	MP-15

Original-Prüfungsaufgaben – Hörverstehen

Schriftliche Abiturprüfung 2021

Teil I: *Listening comprehension*	2021-1
Lösungen	2021-5

Schriftliche Abiturprüfung 2022

Teil I: *Listening comprehension*	2022-1
Lösungen	2022-5

Schriftliche Abiturprüfung 2023 .... www.stark-verlag.de/mystark

Sobald die Original-Prüfungsaufgaben 2023 zum Hörverstehen freigegeben sind, können Sie darauf über die Plattform MyStark zugreifen (Zugangscode auf der Umschlaginnenseite vorne im Buch).

Hördateien

Übungsaufgaben 1–8
Offizielle Musterprüfung
Abiturprüfung 2021–2023

Hinweis: Die **MP3-Dateien** finden Sie ebenfalls auf der Plattform **MyStark**.

Texte ÜA 1-Task 1 und ÜA 2-Task 1 + 4 gesprochen von: Eva Adelseck, Daniel Beaver, Clare Gnasmüller, Daniel Holzberg, Veronica Stivala

Aufgaben und Lösungen verfasst von:

Birte Bökel:	Übungsaufgabe 1 zum Prüfungsteil Lesen und Schreiben
Karin Feldner:	Übungsaufgabe 2 zum Prüfungsteil Lesen und Schreiben
Rainer Jacob:	Übungsaufgabe 3 und 4 zum Prüfungsteil Lesen und Schreiben Lösungen zur offiziellen Musterprüfung (Set 1 und Kommunikationsprüfung)
Dorothée Just:	Übungsaufgaben zum Hörverstehen Lösungen zur offiziellen Musterprüfung (Set 2 und Hörverstehen) Lösungen zu den Original-Prüfungsaufgaben (Hörverstehen)

Vorwort

Liebe Abiturientinnen und Abiturienten,

mit dem Jahrgang **2024** werden sich die Aufgabenformate in der **schriftlichen Abiturprüfung** im Beruflichen Gymnasium ändern. Dieser Band bereitet Sie optimal auf die **neuen Aufgabenformate** im Fach Englisch vor.

Damit Sie gut trainiert in Ihr Abitur gehen, stellen wir Ihnen zahlreiche **Übungsaufgaben** zu den Prüfungsteilen **Hörverstehen** sowie **Lesen und Schreiben** bereit. Die Übungsaufgaben umfassen Aufgabenformate und Textsorten, die Ihnen in der Prüfung begegnen können. Anhand der **offiziellen Musterprüfung** können Sie schließlich auch eine komplette Prüfung durcharbeiten.

Im Bereich Hörverstehen eignen sich auch die **Original-Hörverstehensprüfungen** der Jahre **2021 bis 2023** zum Üben, da die Aufgabenformate auch denjenigen in der neuen Prüfung entsprechen.

Sie erhalten außerdem eine Beschreibung der Prüfungsziele sowie konkrete Lerntipps und sprachliche Hilfen für die effektive Vorbereitung. Detaillierte **Hinweise**, sowie im Teil „Lesen und Schreiben" ausführliche **Beispiellösungen**, führen Sie an die erfolgreiche Bearbeitung der Aufgaben heran.

Lernen Sie gerne am PC, Tablet oder Smartphone? Auf den nächsten Seiten finden Sie Hinweise zu den digitalen Zusätzen zu diesem Band

Sollten nach Erscheinen dieses Bandes noch wichtige Änderungen in der Abitur-Prüfung vom Kultusministerium bekannt gegeben werden, finden Sie aktuelle Informationen dazu ebenfalls auf der Plattform MyStark.

Viel Erfolg wünschen Ihnen

Rainer Jacob und Dorothée Just

Hinweise zu den digitalen Zusätzen

Auf alle digitalen Zusätze können Sie online über die Plattform **MyStark** zugreifen. Ihren persönlichen Zugangscode finden Sie auf der Umschlaginnenseite vorne im Buch.

PDF der Original-Prüfungsaufgaben 2023

Um Ihnen die Hörverstehensaufgaben der Prüfung 2023 schnellstmöglich zur Verfügung stellen zu können, bringen wir sie in digitaler Form heraus. Sobald die Original-Prüfungsaufgaben 2023 zur Veröffentlichung freigegeben sind, können sie auf der Plattform MyStark heruntergeladen werden.

Hördateien

Über die Plattform MyStark können Sie sich außerdem die Hörverstehenstexte der Übungsaufgaben sowie der Abiturprüfungen ab 2021 anhören und zum Offline-Gebrauch herunterladen.

Interaktive Aufgaben

Im interaktiven Training „**Basic Language Skills**" erhalten Sie Zugriff auf zahlreiche **interaktive Aufgaben** zu Grundlagen wie Hörverstehen, Leseverstehen und Sprachverwendung im Kontext. Dies sind ganz wichtige „Basics", die Sie für eine gute Sprachbeherrschung brauchen.

Das Prüfungstraining „Basic Language Skills" bietet Ihnen:

- „**Listening**" – authentische Hörtexte mit vielfältigen Aufgaben, die Ihr Hörverstehen testen
- „**Reading**" – abwechslungsreiche Lesetexte und dazugehörige Aufgaben

- **„English in Use"** mit gemischten Aufgaben rund um den Gebrauch der englischen Sprache
- Alle Aufgaben sind interaktiv, d. h., Sie können sie direkt am PC bearbeiten und erhalten sofort eine Rückmeldung zu Ihren Antworten.

Lernvideos

Mithilfe der **Lernvideos zum richtigen Umgang mit Textaufgaben** können Sie sich optimal auf die Anforderungen in diesem Bereich vorbereiten. Am Beispiel von zwei Texten mit je drei Aufgabenstellungen wird gezeigt, wie man an Textaufgaben herangeht und sie erfolgreich löst.

Die Lernvideos beinhalten:
- **Schritt-für-Schritt-Anleitungen** zum richtigen Vorgehen anhand exemplarischer Aufgabenstellungen
- **Sachtext** als Grundlage
- nützliche Hinweise zu **häufigen Operatoren** und **Zieltextsorten**

Web-App „MindCards"

Mit der Web-App „**MindCards**" können Sie am Smartphone Vokabeln lernen. Auf diesen interaktiven Karteikarten finden Sie hilfreiche Wendungen, die Sie beim Schreiben von Texten oder im mündlichen Sprachgebrauch einsetzen können.

Scannen Sie einfach die QR-Codes oder verwenden Sie folgende Links, um zu den „MindCards" zu gelangen:
https://www.stark-verlag.de/mindcards/writing-2
https://www.stark-verlag.de/mindcards/speaking-2

Writing

Speaking

Kurzgrammatik

In der Kurzgrammatik werden alle wichtigen grammatischen Themen knapp erläutert und an Beispielsätzen veranschaulicht. Sie können die Kurzgrammatik als pdf herunterladen.

HINWEISE UND TIPPS

Hinweise und Tipps zur Abiturprüfung

1 Struktur der schriftlichen Abiturprüfung

Die **schriftliche Prüfung** besteht aus einem **schriftlichen Teil** und einer **Kommunikationsprüfung**.
Die Arbeitszeit für den schriftlichen Teil beträgt 240 Minuten und es können insgesamt 60 Verrechnungspunkte erreicht werden. Als Hilfsmittel steht Ihnen ein einsprachiges Wörterbuch zur Verfügung. Damit Sie von dieser Möglichkeit sinnvoll Gebrauch machen können, ist es nötig, dass Sie sich mit dem an Ihrer Schule zugelassenen Lexikon vertraut machen und die Verwendung einüben.
Die Aufgaben im schriftlichen Teil sind folgendermaßen gegliedert:
- Teil I: Hörverstehen
- Teil II: Lesen und Schreiben

Teil I: Hörverstehen
Bei den Hörtexten in der schriftlichen Prüfung handelt es sich um authentische monologische oder dialogische Texte. Die Texte werden immer zweimal vorgespielt. Es kann sich dabei z. B. um Podcasts, Interviews oder Radioreportagen handeln. Anhand der dazugehörigen Aufgaben wird geprüft, ob Sie die Hauptaussagen eines Hörtextes verstehen (globales Hören – *listening for the gist*) oder die Detailaussagen (selektives Hören – *listening for detail*), aber auch, ob Sie die implizite Bedeutung eines Textes erschließen können (inferierendes Hören – *infer meaning*).

Teil II: Lesen und Schreiben
Die Aufgaben beziehen sich auf einen längeren englischen Sachtext von maximal 800 Wörtern. In diesem Teil gibt es **zwei Sets** (mit jeweils einem eigenen Lesetext) zur Auswahl, die beide in drei Aufgaben unterteilt sind. Thematisch beziehen sich die Aufgaben auf die Lehrplaneinheiten Landeskunde und Arbeitswelt. Zu den wichtigsten Themen gehören unter anderem:

- Umwelt, Energie, Ressourcen
  z. B. *global warming*, Biodiversität, Müll und Recycling, Arten der Energiegewinnung, Wasserknappheit, Rohstoffe
- Aktuelle Technologien/vernetzte Gesellschaft
  z. B. Gentechnik, Lebensmittelproduktion, moderne Produktionsmethoden, Digitalisierung und Automatisierung (*smart homes*, *drones*, CCTV, *Internet of Things*, *robots*), *AI*
- Konsum
  z. B. Werbung, Kommunikations- und Konsumverhalten, soziale, wirtschaftliche und ethische Fragestellungen
- USA: historische Entwicklung und aktuelle Politik
  z. B. Besiedlung und Entstehung, *American Dream*, politische, wirtschaftliche und militärische Rolle der USA in der modernen Welt
- UK: historische Entwicklung und aktuelle Politik
  z. B. Empire, Commonwealth, Beziehung zur EU, Identität im gesellschaftlichen Spannungsfeld
  z. B. *multi-cultural society*, nationale Stereotypen, soziale Schichten, ethnische Gruppen, Minderheiten, *acculturation versus parallel societies*
- Chancen und Herausforderungen in der Arbeitswelt
  Globalisierung, z. B. Entwicklung der Globalisierung, globale Arbeitsteilung, *free trade vs. protectionism*
  Internationale Begegnungen im beruflichen Umfeld (z. B. Umgangsformen, *small talk*), kulturelle Heterogenität am Arbeitsplatz
  Bedeutung der interkulturellen Kompetenz
- Soziale Fragestellungen/Arbeitskultur
  z. B. Unterschiede bei der Entlohnung von Arbeit (*gender gap, pay gap, gap between rich and poor*), Arbeitnehmerrechte, Arbeitslosigkeit
  work-life-balance, teleworking

Zur intensiven Vorbereitung auf diese Themenbereiche können Sie das Abitur-Skript Englisch (Best.-Nr. 10546S1) nutzen. Zur Erweiterung und Festigung des themenspezifischen Wortschatzes eignet sich der Band „Englisch-KOMPAKT Wortschatz Oberstufe" (Best.-Nr. 90462D).

Teil III: Sprechen (Kommunikationsprüfung)

Der dritte Teil der Abiturprüfung im Fach Englisch ist eine mündliche Prüfung, die **Kommunikationsprüfung**, die als Einzelprüfung oder Zweierprüfung (Tandemprüfung) abgenommen werden kann. Sie findet im 4. Schuljahr statt und muss vor Bekanntgabe der Ergebnisse der schriftlichen Prüfung abgeschlossen sein. Zur Vorbereitung erhalten Sie Material, das als Grundlage für die Prüfung dient, z. B. ein Zitat, eine Karikatur, eine Statistik oder ein Foto. In der Vorbereitungszeit für die Einzel- sowie die Tandemprüfung wird nur für den monologischen Teil Material bereitgestellt (in der Tandemprüfung jeweils unterschiedliches Material). Thematisch beziehen sich die

Materialien auf den Lehrplan der Jahrgangsstufen 1 und 2. In der Vorbereitungsphase können Sie ein ein- oder zweisprachiges Wörterbuch verwenden.

Die Prüfung besteht aus zwei Teilen. Im ersten sollen Sie sich ungefähr fünf Minuten lang über das Material, das Sie zur Vorbereitung bekommen haben, frei äußern. Dieses monologische Sprechen fällt nicht immer leicht, wenn man es nicht gewohnt ist. Daher empfiehlt es sich, die freie Rede vorher zu üben, da im Unterricht hierfür nicht immer genügend Zeit zur Verfügung steht. Vor allem sollten Sie sich davon lösen, auf eine Reaktion oder eine Frage, in diesem Fall der prüfenden Lehrkraft, zu warten.

An den ersten Teil schließt sich die zweite Sequenz an, das dialogische Sprechen. Sie sprechen mit der Lehrkraft (bei der Tandemprüfung zusätzlich mit einem Mitschüler oder einer Mitschülerin) über den Sachverhalt, den die Materialien zum Thema haben. Insgesamt dauert die Kommunikationsprüfung ungefähr 15 Minuten. Wenn Sie sich zu zweit prüfen lassen, sind 20 Minuten Prüfungszeit vorgesehen.

 Eine Vielzahl hilfreicher Wendungen zum Bereich „Sprechen" enthalten unsere MindCards, auf die Sie u. a. über nebenstehenden QR-Code Zugriff haben.

2 Gewichtung der einzelnen Prüfungsteile

In der schriftlichen Prüfung werden die einzelnen Prüfungsteile folgendermaßen gewichtet:

Hören	20 %		
Lesen und Schreiben	55 %	**Aufgabe 1:** Integrierte Aufgabe zum Leseverstehen	~25 %
		Aufgabe 2: Textanalyse	~35 %
		Aufgabe 3:	40 %
		Aufgabe 3.1: Erörterung / Stellungnahme	
		oder	
		Aufgabe 3.2: kreative Schreibaufgabe	
Sprechen (Kommunikationsprüfung)	25 %		

Auf Grundlage der Bildungsstandards werden in den einzelnen Prüfungsteilen Aufgaben zu allen drei Anforderungsbereichen gestellt. Im Abitur des Beruflichen Gymnasiums werden dabei die Anforderungsbereiche I und II insgesamt stärker gewichtet. So werden im Bereich „Lesen und Schreiben" die beiden ersten Teilaufgaben zusammen höher gewichtet als die dritte Teilaufgabe. In allen drei Aufgaben des Teils „Lesen und Schreiben" wird die Sprache mit 60 % und der Inhalt mit 40 % gewichtet. Achten Sie deshalb besonders auf Ihre sprachliche Leistung, da Sie hier die meisten Punkte erreichen und damit eine gute Note erzielen können.

3 Praxistipps und sprachliche Hilfen zu den Aufgaben

Bei den Bildungsstandards der Oberstufe unterscheidet man folgende drei Anforderungsbereiche:
- Der Bereich I umfasst Aufgabenstellungen, mit denen das Textverstehen überprüft wird,
- der Bereich II verlangt eine weitergehende Analyse und
- der Bereich III schließlich fordert eine Wertung oder selbstständige Gestaltung der angesprochenen Thematik.

In der schriftlichen Abiturprüfung werden die Anforderungsbereiche I und II im Teil „Hörverstehen" sowie im Teil „Lesen und Schreiben" abgeprüft. Aufgabe 3 im Teil „Lesen und Schreiben" entspricht dem Anforderungsbereich III.

Hörverstehen

Die Aufgabenformate zum Hörverstehen können geschlossen (z. B. *Multiple Matching*, *Multiple Choice*) oder auch halboffen sein (z. B. Kurzantworten). Innerhalb eines Aufgabenteils kann es auch zum Wechsel zwischen den Aufgabenformaten kommen.
Bei den **Multiple Matching-Aufgaben** müssen Sie Aussagen aus dem Hörtext z. B. bestimmten Personen, die im Text vorkommen, zuordnen. Beachten Sie, dass manchmal mehr Aussagen vorgegeben sind als nötig.
Bei den **Multiple Choice-Aufgaben** sollen Sie die richtige Lösung aus mehreren vorgegebenen Möglichkeiten auswählen. Hier kann es sein, dass auch mehr als eine Antwortmöglichkeit richtig ist. Damit die Aufgabe als richtig gelöst gilt, müssen alle korrekten Alternativen angekreuzt sein.
Aufgabentypen wie **Kurzantworten** und **Satzergänzungen** sind halboffene Formate, bei denen Sie die Lösungen in Stichpunkten notieren. Rechtschreib- und Grammatikfehler werden dabei nicht gewertet, sie dürfen jedoch den Sinn nicht entstellen.
Am besten bereiten Sie sich auf den Teil „Hörverstehen" vor, indem Sie viel auf Englisch hören bzw. sich ansehen. Versuchen Sie, Filme oder Serien im englischen Original anzuschauen – als Hilfe können Sie anfangs auch die deutschen oder englischen Untertitel einstellen. Hören Sie auch Podcasts und Nachrichten auf Englisch, z. B. von der BBC oder von VoA (Voice of America). Auch das Hören englischsprachiger Songs hilft, das Hörverstehen zu schulen. Versuchen Sie, den Inhalt zu verstehen, indem Sie den Text in Stichworten mitschreiben oder Wordwebs anlegen. Dabei können Sie gleichzeitig Ihren Wortschatz erweitern und z. B. Synonyme und Antonyme sammeln und lernen. Mithilfe der interaktiven Hörverstehensaufgaben, die in diesem Buch enthalten sind, können Sie Ihr Hörverstehen ebenfalls trainieren.

Lesen und Schreiben

Hier müssen Sie unter Beweis stellen, dass Sie längere authentische Texte verstehen, indem Sie dem Text Hauptaussagen und Einzelinformationen entnehmen und diese in thematische Zusammenhänge einordnen können. Sie sollen ebenfalls in der Lage sein, implizite Aussagen zu erschließen und auch zusätzliches Wissen heranzuziehen. In Aufgabe 3 wird von Ihnen verlangt, dass Sie über den Lesetext hinaus adressatengerecht und textsortenspezifisch einen eigenen Text verfassen.

Aufgabe 1: Integrierte Aufgabe zum Leseverstehen

Hier wird überprüft, ob Sie den Inhalt des englischen Sachtextes verstanden haben. Sie sollen dabei bestimmte, in der Aufgabenstellung geforderte Aspekte des Textes in eigenen Worten zusammenfassen. Achten Sie dabei immer auf den jeweiligen Operator. **Operatoren** definieren die Aufgabenstellung und die damit verbundenen Anforderungen. Diese Aufgabe deckt den Anforderungsbereich I ab, der u. a. folgende Operatoren umfassen kann:

Operator	Erklärung	Beispiel
Describe ...	Genaue Beschreibung z. B. einer Person, einer Entwicklung oder Situation	*Describe the advantages and disadvantages of globalisation.*
Outline ...	Grobe Wiedergabe wesentlicher inhaltlicher Aspekte	*Outline the difficulties faced by journalists when trying to present objective news.*
Point out ...	Herausfiltern und Erklären bestimmter Informationen zu einem Aspekt.	*Point out the challenges faced by women in their workplace.*
Present ...	Strukturierte Wiedergabe z. B. einer Situation oder eines Ergebnisses	*Present the findings of the EU Commission regarding population growth since the turn of the century.*
State ...	Kurze und knappe Wiedergabe eines Sachverhalts oder eines wesentlichen Aspekts davon	*State the reasons of the judges to rule against the right of abortion.*
Summarise ...	Inhaltliche Zusammenfassung eines Textes bzw. eines bestimmten Aspekts, der im Text erwähnt wird	*Summarise the UN's findings on food security in emerging economies.*

Aufgabe 2: Textanalyse

Auch bei dieser Aufgabe dient der Lesetext als Grundlage. Die Aufgabenstellung erfordert nun jedoch eine tiefere Beschäftigung mit dem Text (Anforderungsbereich II), d. h., eine Textanalyse unter Beachtung von Struktur und sprachlichen Mitteln. Hier kann es u. a. darum gehen, die Position des Autors/der Autorin unter Verdeutlichung von (rhetorischen) Gestaltungsmitteln herauszuarbeiten. Zum Anforderungsbereich II gehören u. a. folgende Operatoren:

Operator	Erklärung	Beispiel
Analyse ... / *Examine ...*	Detaillierte Analyse des Textes auf bestimmte Aspekte	*Analyse the author's attitude towards his home country and the means he uses to convey it. / Examine the opposing views on the UK's decision to leave the EU.*
Characterise ...	Detaillierte Beschreibung eines Sachverhalts oder einer Figur	*Characterise the overall situation of African Americans in the 1960s.*
Compare ...	Herausstellen von Unterschieden und Gemeinsamkeiten bzw. Ähnlichkeiten von Sachverhalten und Figuren	*Compare the differing attitudes of the presidential candidates towards climate change.*
Contrast ...	Herausarbeiten von Unterschieden bei Figuren und Sachverhalten	*Contrast the views of the Republican and Democratic Party regarding immigration.*
Explain ...	Beschreibung von Sachverhalten oder bestimmten Aspekten davon und Benennung von Ursachen oder Folgen	*Explain the reasons for the increase in life expectancy in wealthy industrialised nations.*
Illustrate ...	Veranschaulichung eines Sachverhalts anhand von Beispielen aus dem Text	*Illustrate the damages caused by plastic pollution.*
Interpret ...	Herausarbeiten der Bedeutung, Funktion oder Botschaft eines Textes oder Bildes etc.	*Interpret the message the author wishes to convey.*

Aufgabe 3: Erörterung/Stellungnahme *oder* kreative Schreibaufgabe

Hier haben Sie die Auswahl zwischen zwei verschiedenen Aufgaben, die die Anforderungsbereiche II und III abdecken.

Aufgabe 3.1 ist text- und materialbezogen und erfordert eine argumentierende oder wertende Stellungnahme. Als Grundlage können z. B. neben einem Zitat aus dem Text weitere Materialien wie eine Grafik, eine Statistik oder eine Karikatur dienen. Folgende Operatoren können Ihnen hier begegnen:

Operator	Erklärung	Beispiel
Assess ... / *Evaluate ...*	Fundierte Bewertung eines Sachverhalts; bei „evaluate" auch Formulierung eines abschließenden Urteils	*Assess how people's background influences their aims and ambitions. / Evaluate the importance of the Commonwealth today.*
Comment on ...	Oft durch Textbelege gestütztes, begründetes Darlegen der eigenen Meinung	*"The purpose of development aid is to develop the export markets of the industrialised countries." Comment on this statement.*

Discuss ...	Beleuchtung eines Themas mit Pro- und Kontraargumenten inklusive abschließender begründeter Meinungsäußerung	*Discuss the benefits and harms of artificial intelligence.*

Bei **Aufgabe 3.2** handelt es sich um eine kreative Schreibaufgabe, die sich im weiteren Sinn auf die Thematik das Ausgangstextes bezieht. Hier soll jedoch über den Text hinausgehendes Wissen einfließen. Sie verfassen dabei einen zusammenhängenden und strukturierten Text (z. B. eine Rede oder einen Blog), der den in der Aufgabenstellung genannten Kontext und ggf. die Adressaten und Adressatinnen berücksichtigt.

Überlegen Sie sich gut, welche der beiden Alternativen in Aufgabe 3 Sie bearbeiten wollen. Entscheidend ist, dass Sie sich klarmachen, was Ihnen besser liegt – eine text- und materialbezogene Stellungnahme oder eine kreative Schreibaufgabe, bei der Sie freier formulieren können, aber mehr eigenes Hintergrundwissen heranziehen müssen. Gehen Sie daher vor der Prüfung auch die einzelnen Themenbereiche des Lehrplans durch und eignen Sie sich wichtige Aspekte der jeweiligen Themen an. Ihre Lösung soll jedoch nicht nur inhaltlich, sondern auch sprachlich überzeugen, wobei die sprachliche Umsetzung mit 60 % sogar höher gewichtet wird. Hier sollen Sie beweisen, dass Sie über die sprachlichen Mittel verfügen, einen Sachverhalt zu bewerten bzw. eine Meinung überzeugend zu vertreten. Sie müssen daher nicht nur auf den Inhalt Ihrer Lösung achten, sondern auch dem sinnvollen Aufbau und der sprachlichen Formulierung Beachtung schenken. Ob Sie sich angemessen und differenziert ausdrücken können, fällt hier besonders ins Gewicht. Reaktivieren Sie den Wortschatz, der zum Thema gehört, und zeigen Sie bei Ihrer Wortwahl, dass Sie das relevante Vokabular einsetzen können. In diesem Zusammenhang sollten Sie das Wörterbuch sinnvoll nutzen. Ebenfalls stark ins Gewicht fällt, inwiefern es Ihnen gelingt, eine zusammenhängende Darstellung zu verfassen. Dazu sollten Sie u. a. die entsprechenden Verknüpfungen *(connectives, linkage words)* zwischen Satzteilen und Sätzen sinnvoll und logisch einsetzen.

Hinweise und Tipps zu Inhalt und Sprache
Allgemeine Tipps
- nicht einseitig auf inhaltliche Aspekte konzentrieren
- klare, einfache (nicht „simple") Sätze formulieren
- Wiederholungen sowohl inhaltlich als auch sprachlich vermeiden: Synonyme oder Umschreibungen verwenden
- Bezüge deutlich machen (wer ist „it", „they"?)
- „etc." und „and so on" vermeiden
- Satzverknüpfungen *(linkage words, connectives)* verwenden, um die Einzelsätze miteinander zu verbinden
- Zeit gut einteilen, um Formulierungen überprüfen zu können

Beispiele für Satzverknüpfungen *(connectives, linkage words)*

Aussageabsicht	Satzverknüpfung
einen Gedanken hinzufügen:	*in addition, further, furthermore, also, besides, in the same way*
das Gegenteil ausdrücken:	*yet, however, on the other hand, on the contrary, in contrast, in spite of*
einen Vergleich anstellen:	*similarly, in the same way, likewise*
eine Folgerung ausdrücken:	*consequently, therefore, as a result*
eine Einräumung ausdrücken:	*although, though, even if, after all, in any case*
eine zeitliche Verknüpfung herstellen:	*after, before, while, eventually, recently, lately, at last, in the end, in the past, when, as soon as*
eine Begründung anführen:	*therefore, that is why, for this reason, because, since*
eine Bedingung ausdrücken:	*if, unless, provided that, in case that*
ein Beispiel anführen:	*for example, for instance, in other words*
die Reihenfolge verdeutlichen:	*first, second, next, finally, in the end*
einen Gedanken neu formulieren:	*in other words, that means, that is, that is to say*
einen Gedankengang abschließen:	*in conclusion, in brief, in short, on the whole*

Weitere Beispiele für hilfreiche Wendungen

Aussageabsicht	Formulierung
Argumente ordnen:	*First of all / To begin with I would like to ...* *Another (significant) reason/advantage/consequence is ...* *This brings us to the question of whether ...* *In addition / Moreover / Besides / Furthermore you cannot deny that ...* *It is worth stating at this point that ...* *But above all ...*
die eigene Meinung ausdrücken:	*It seems to me ... / It has been my experience ...* *As far as I can see ... / The way I see it ... / My own view of that is ...* *I am afraid the author is wrong in saying/claiming ...* *I maintain that ... / I am convinced that ...* *In my opinion / To my mind you can say that/accept that ...* *My main argument/my point is that ...* *Surely/Obviously it is wrong to say that ...*

auf die Gegenmeinung eingehen:	*All the same / Nevertheless it is wrong to say that ...* *Contrary to public belief / the popular idea / notion ...* *Despite all those arguments we still face the problem that ...* *In contrast to / As opposed to ... I think ...* *It is true that ... but it is definitely wrong to say that ...* *We mustn't forget, however, that ...*
eine logische Folgerung ziehen:	*All this shows it is unwise to assume that ...* *From all this follows that ...* *So / Therefore / That is why we can't assume that ...*
einen Schluss formulieren:	*All in all, I therefore reject the view that ...* *In sum / In brief I cannot accept the suggestion that ...* *To conclude / In conclusion / As a result you can safely say that ...* *Weighing the pros and cons one comes to the conclusion that ...*

 Viele weitere hilfreiche Wendungen zum Bereich „Schreiben" enthalten übrigens unsere MindCards, auf die Sie u. a. über nebenstehenden QR-Code Zugriff haben.

Tipp Auch wenn sich die Aufgabenstellung im Detail je nach Text unterscheidet, bleibt die grundsätzliche Vorgehensweise bei den jeweiligen Operatoren gleich. In den **Videos** auf der Plattform **MyStark** (Zugangscode vorne im Buch) erklären wir Ihnen, wie Sie bei den wichtigsten Operatoren im Bereich Schreiben vorgehen müssen. Außerdem erfahren Sie etwas zu häufigen Zieltextformaten wie z. B. Leserbrief oder Blogeintrag.

ÜBUNGSAUFGABEN

Hörverstehen · Übungsaufgabe 1
Baden-Württemberg · Berufliches Gymnasium · Englisch

Renting a house or apartment

Listen to four young people talking about renting a house or apartment. Match each speaker (1 to 4) with one of the statements (A to G) by putting the corresponding letter into the correct box. For each speaker there is only one correct answer. There are three more options than you need.

The speaker …

A was happy that they found a cheap, cosy apartment with a spacious garden and a big office.

B had a problem with the owner of the house and told him they were moving out.

C first thought they found their dream house, but now regrets the decision to move in.

D isn't renting yet and feels as if the situation will never improve.

E did something new by renting out a flat for holiday-makers.

F found a very caring landlord who put a lot of effort into making the apartment homelike before they moved in.

G moved back home in order to be able to afford the high costs of living.

Speaker	1	2	3	4
Statement				

Lösungen

Transcript — Renting a house or apartment

Speaker 1

We saw the ad in the summer, in about July, I think, but we weren't really serious about moving then so we didn't even go and see it. It wasn't until November when they re-advertised it that we got in touch with the agency and had a look. They'd put the price down since the summer too, I suppose because it had been empty so long, so that made it more affordable for us which helped us make up our minds. It was perfect – a bigger garden for the kids and enough space for an office. In winter it was lovely, very cosy, in fact, which is important to me as I really feel the cold, whereas my husband will open a window when it's minus temperatures outside! Anyway, in July when summer really started and we had that heatwave, we understood why no one had wanted to rent it over summer. It was boiling! All those lovely big windows that made the flat so light and open were like a greenhouse as soon as it got warmer. From about 8 in the morning until 7 in the evening, it was like living in a sauna! We couldn't stand being at home, and weekends were especially bad. No air conditioning, of course. If only we'd gone to see it when it was first advertised in July, we'd never have moved in!

Speaker 2

I always rent apartments when I go on holiday, rather than staying in hotels. Hotels are so impersonal, aren't they? This way you get to feel like you really live in the place you're visiting. It's the first time I've done it the other way round, though, and rented out my place … but it seemed like a good way of making some extra money. The website is really easy to use and they only charge five per cent commission, which is lower than a lot of the other holiday rental sites. It's all about the photos and the reviews. Get the photos right and the place can look really upmarket and spacious, but you don't want to make it look too much better than it really is or you end up with a bad review. It's better to undersell and overdeliver so guests are pleasantly surprised and leave an extra positive review. So far, I'm averaging three stars because of one bad review that brought my average down from four and a half stars, but hopefully I'll get it back up during the busy season.

Speaker 3

Buying a house seems so far out of my reach it's almost impossible, as it is for loads of people my age these days. My parents always told me renting was throwing money away, but it was different in their day. Then people could afford to buy a house on a normal salary, but nowadays house prices are so high and no bank will look at you unless you've got a huge deposit. The problem with my dream of buying is that it's never going to come true. Not unless my parents help me out, but I've got two sisters and we're all in the same position. At least they've both got good jobs. Not good enough to buy a house, but at least they can afford to rent places of their own in nice areas. I just don't earn enough to rent around here. Even if I get promoted to manager, it'll be tough to find somewhere unless I share, and call me fussy, but there aren't that many people I want to share a bathroom and kitchen with. Some days I think I'll be stuck living with my parents forever – even renting is like a dream to me.

Speaker 4
At first our landlord was really helpful, couldn't do enough for us. You hear stories of nightmare landlords and we felt like we were really lucky, or so we thought anyway. He redecorated the whole place, from top to bottom, and let us keep all the bills in his name so we didn't have the bother of contacting all the companies ourselves. He even offered to come round and do the gardening as he knew we both worked long hours and might not have time. That's where the problems started now I look back. Then he'd pop round 'just to check everything's OK for you' once a month, then twice a month. Soon he was coming every week with some excuse or other. In the beginning we'd invite him in for tea, but it was only encouraging him, so when we realised, we'd try to have the conversation on the doorstep instead. It got so bad we pretended to be on our way out if we saw him coming up the path. We'd grab our coats and walk round the block until he'd gone. I don't know if he was just lonely or just didn't trust us not to ruin his precious house. In the end we gave our notice and found somewhere else. It's a shame because we really loved that house, but at least it's more peaceful in the new place.

Adapted from: British Council, https://learnenglish.britishcouncil.org/skills/listening/advanced-c1/renting-a-house

> **TIPP**
>
> This task tests your ability to grasp the general content of a text, so you need to pick out the relevant information. Read the statements carefully – in the texts synonyms are used, which may distract you. While listening, do not focus on every single word. Content is often repeated in several ways and with different expressions.
>
> – **zu Speaker 1 – C:** "It was perfect ..." (l. 5), "If only we'd gone to see it when it was first advertised in July, we'd never have moved in!" (ll. 13 f.)
> The speaker first mentions her positive impression of the flat (e. g. ll. 6 f.: "bigger garden", "enough space", "cosy"), which could hint at statement A, but later she clearly points out that they "couldn't stand being at home" (ll. 12 f.)
>
> – **zu Speaker 2 – E:** "It's the first time I've done it the other way round, though, and rented out my place ..." (ll. 17 f.) Here, the mentioning of "renting out" is the key to the correct solution.

- **zu Speaker 3 – D:** "Some days I think I'll be stuck living with my parents forever – even renting is like a dream to me." (ll. 37 f.)
  The speaker still seems to live with her parents ("stuck living with my parents") and does not mention moving back in with them (as in statement G).
  Moreover, she is not talking about the high costs of living in general (as also mentioned in statement G), but about high rents and the impossibility of buying a house.
- **zu Speaker 4 – B:** "In the end we gave our notice and found somewhere else." (l. 51) Although the speaker talks about a caring landlord, which could point towards sentence F, he later talks about "problems" (l. 44) and that "it got so bad" (l. 48).

Speaker	1	2	3	4
Statement	C	E	D	B

Hörverstehen • Übungsaufgabe 2
Baden-Württemberg • Berufliches Gymnasium • Englisch

| Floodings in the UK |

Listen to the podcast about flooding in the UK by Prof. Carolyn Roberts.
While listening, tick (✓) the correct answer (a, b, c or d).
There is only one correct answer.

1 One main issue which is <u>not</u> mentioned concerning flooding in the UK is …
   a ☐ the means to deal with floods.
   b ☐ matters of trade and commerce.
   c ☐ the financial damage caused by floods.

2 The speaker says that …
   a ☐ flooding is only caused by humans.
   b ☐ climate change makes floods occur twice a year on average.
   c ☐ a combination of human and natural influences causes floods.

3 There are different types of flooding Prof. Roberts mentions. The type of flooding which is most dangerous to humans is …
   a ☐ flooding from rivers.
   b ☐ ground water flooding.
   c ☐ flooding that occurs on the seashore.

4 The event which will most likely affect London is …
   a ☐ heavy rainfall flooding the city.
   b ☐ the bursting of the flood barriers.
   c ☐ ground water pushing to the surface.

5 The average annual costs of flooding in the UK …
   a ☐ amount to several billion pounds.
   b ☐ will increase by billions of pounds every year.
   c ☐ will decrease because it will rain less because of global warming.

6 Limiting global warming to an average of 2 degrees …
- **a** ☐ won't have any effect.
- **b** ☐ will have a huge impact on how much damage is caused by flooding.
- **c** ☐ will reduce the impact of flooding in the UK but not in other parts of the world.

7 The statement that describes the impact of a 4-degree change in the atmosphere:
- **a** ☐ floods will be more deadly
- **b** ☐ the UK will face serious economic damage
- **c** ☐ the outcome of flooding will be more severe

8 The objective of this podcast is to …
- **a** ☐ explain climate change in general.
- **b** ☐ spread awareness of the connection between floods and global warming.
- **c** ☐ promote further scientific research on floodings in the United Kingdom.

Lösungen

Transcript — Floodings in the UK

The UK has a series of problems associated with flooding. One of them is to do with the physical background of the flooding itself, so the things that are creating the flooding – intense rainfall, high windspeeds in oceans, sea levels, storminess and so on. The other significant element is how we manage it, what we do about managing both the water and the damage that the water creates when it gets into inappropriate places like people's living rooms and so on. The third element is to do with the ways things are shifting as the climate shifts, so that the risks are becoming more intense, particularly in certain parts of the country. So it's a threefold, complex and very wicked problem if you like.

Climate change is part of what we're talking about, flooding is a natural phenomenon – rivers have always overtopped their banks (they never 'burst' their banks or almost never). We have altered the environment very significantly anyway with the things we do, the way we farm, the way we constrain rivers and so on, so it's a mixture of a naturally induced phenomenon (flooding always happens) and the problem of the way we behave in circumstances close to the rivers, close to the coast. [...]

There are three [sic] types of flooding that are really important. The most important in terms of the cost and the number of people at risk is undoubtedly flooding from rivers. So the larger rivers – the Ouse in Yorkshire, the Severn, parts of the Thames above London and so on – those are areas of some significance (there are others as well).

The next most significant in terms of economic costs is coastal flooding. And there we're talking about the areas around East Anglia, but also the Thames Estuary and areas of Essex and Kent and some smaller areas in Lincolnshire, but there are isolated areas all over the place where we have vulnerable bits of infrastructure.

And the other important area of flooding is flooding from surface water run-off from urban areas where we got run-off, well actually not just in urban areas, in the fields immediately around urban areas where we got either impermeable surfaces or we got agricultural land that's rather badly managed and generates a lot of run-off. So those are very localised and responsive to intense rain, and all the climate models suggest that's going to happen more frequently. [...]

The last kind of flooding actually that has some significance particularly in and around London is ground water flooding – clear water flooding we call it – and that's caused by generally wet periods rather than intense rain but when water levels rise and get into areas where they are not supposed to be. That's a bit more insidious but it's still quite significant actually.

The total costs at the moment are in the billions of pounds a year on average and as we go forward into the future they become even more significant. So, it's worth doing something about, I think. [...]

Keeping average global temperature changes to around 2 degrees will dramatically avert some of the damage from flooding that would occur should we not be able to do that. Once you start getting to 4 degrees of change you are into much more serious

consequences in terms of flooding. As the atmosphere heats up, everything tends to move more quickly – the atmosphere becomes more volatile, the sea level rises, you get more rainstorms and so on – at least in the UK where we sit in relation to the position of the jet stream. Other places in the globe will experience things differently,
45 but certainly our experience here in the UK is likely to be one of more extremes, and that's of some consequence.

Carolyn Roberts/Lee Millam: Pod Academy, November 30, 2015. http://podacademy.org/podcasts/the-next-big-flood-britain-underwater/

TIPP

In this task you need to listen for detail and also infer what is meant by the text. It is important that you first read the given tasks and alternatives carefully in order to recognise the correct solution while listening to the text.
In general, many aspects are repeated once or sometimes twice in other words or with examples. This will also help you when parts of the text are mumbled or maybe spoken too fast, so listen closely in order to understand what is said.

- **Zu 1:** The issue here is to be able to understand what is meant by the problems mentioned. Although the speaker talks about the "economic costs" of flooding (l. 20), issues concerning trade and commerce are not mentioned explicitly. You should keep to the actual meaning of the words and not jump to conclusions too fast.

- **Zu 2:** Here it helps to understand technical terms and more sophisticated wording (e. g. "induced" or "circumstances"), but the correct solution can also be found without knowing these phrases: "We have altered the environment very significantly […] with the things we do, the way we farm, the way we constrain rivers and so on, so it's a mixture of a naturally induced phenomenon (flooding always happens) and the problem of the way we behave in circumstances close to the rivers, close to the coast." (ll. 12 ff.)

- **Zu 3:** You need to choose the type of flooding most dangerous to humans. Other dangers are also mentioned but are not relevant to the task.
"The most important – both in cost terms and the number of people at risk is undoubtedly flooding from rivers." (ll. 16 f.)

- **Zu 4:** Listen closely for the key words "London" and "ground water". "When water levels rise" is rephrased in the task with "ground water pushing to the surface": "The last kind of flooding […] that has some significance particularly in and around London is ground water flooding […] and that's caused by generally wet periods rather than intense rain but when water levels rise and get into areas where they are not supposed to be." (ll. 30 ff.)

- **Zu 5:** The words "average" and "annual" (= "a year") give you the hint here: "The total costs at the moment are in the <u>billions of pounds a year on average</u> and as we go forward into the future they become even more significant." (ll. 35 f.)
- **Zu 6:** The words "huge impact" hint towards "Keeping average global temperature changes to around 2 degrees <u>will dramatically avert some of the damage from flooding</u> that would occur should we not be able to do that." (ll. 38 ff.)
- **Zu 7:** "Severe" and "serious" can be used as synonyms, but they do not necessarily mean "more deadly" in the sense of more people dying because of flooding. To find the relevant paragraph in the text, listen for the key phrase "4 degrees of change": "Once you start getting to 4 degrees of change you are <u>into much more serious consequences</u> in terms of flooding." (ll. 40 f.)
- **Zu 8:** This task tests your general understanding of what was said. If you are not sure whether you have ticked the correct solution, read the other tasks again and think about what could match the general statements given. This is best done after the second listening.

1 One main issue which is <u>not</u> mentioned concerning flooding in the UK is …
   b ✓ matters of trade and commerce.

2 The speaker says that …
   c ✓ a combination of human and natural influences causes floods.

3 There are different types of flooding, Prof. Roberts mentions. The type of flooding which is most dangerous to humans is …
   a ✓ flooding from rivers.

4 The event which will most likely affect London is …
   c ✓ ground water pushing to the surface.

5 The average annual costs of flooding in the UK …
   a ✓ amount to several billion pounds.

6 Limiting global warming to an average of 2 degrees …
   b ✓ will have a huge impact on how much damage is caused by flooding.

7 The statement that describes the impact of a 4-degree change in the atmosphere:
   c ✓ the outcome of flooding will be more severe

8 The objective of this podcast is to …
   b ✓ spread awareness of the connection between floods and global warming.

Hörverstehen ▪ Übungsaufgabe 3
Baden-Württemberg ▪ Berufliches Gymnasium ▪ Englisch

Happiness by design: Finding pleasure and purpose in everyday life

Listen to the following radio report about finding pleasure and purpose in everyday life. While listening, complete the notes on the points listed on this worksheet. You do not need to write in complete sentences.

1 What happy lives encompass, according to Prof. Dolan:
- _____
- _____

2 Happiness as defined by client 1:
- _____
- _____

3 Three things that make client 2 happy:
- _____
- _____
- _____

4 Two examples given by Prof. Dolan regarding how we could use our time better:
- _____
- _____

5 Reason why people do not act in the right way to be able to be happy:
_____

6 Prof. Dolan's recommendation concerning happiness:
_____

Lösungen

Transcript — Happiness by design: Finding pleasure and purpose in everyday life

Professor Paul Dolan: For me happiness is in our experiences of life. Things that we feel day to day, moment to moment. And I talk about pleasure and purpose. OK, so my name's Paul Dolan, I'm at London School of Economics and my book is called *Happiness by design – Finding pleasure and purpose in everyday life*. So, happy lives are ones that contain some balance; it's not the same for everybody and it's not in equal measure. But some kind of balance between things that we find fun on the one hand and things that we find fulfilling on the other. Well, it is a subjective experience. I think everything ultimately matters because it makes us feel better, so I can describe to you I think the things that I find pleasurable and the things that I find purposeful. And I can also probably give you a good sense of how much I find them pleasurable and how much I find them purposeful. And equally, of course, things that I find painful and things that I find pointless, so I think we are now getting a better insight into the quantitative nature of those elements.

Client 1: Happiness for me is a very ethereal thing, I think. By that I mean that it is very difficult to say what it is, and it can be different, at different stages of my life. But in essence, happiness for me, as I've grown older, is quite a few intangible things, things which make me think that life is worth it, so it's spending time with the people I want to be with, it's not just living from moment to moment but actually just being in the moment and doing the things that are actually most important. So, the places that are really important for me, and often, actually, it's later on that you realise the happiest times. Well, I'm getting better at that.

Professor Paul Dolan: We're getting many observations on many people over many years, and there seems to be something sensible coming through from the answers people give us. We get associations with some things that you would expect them to be associated with, you know, poverty makes people miserable but being rich doesn't make people happier. So, you know, there are some nice insights coming through from this data. Time that we spend with other people that makes us feel nice, time spent on trains and on tubes and on buses, not so nice.

Client 2: The things that make me happy are: spending time with my friends and family, going out for dinner, going to watch my football team play football, playing with my cat.

Professor Paul Dolan: Well, I think how we use our time is absolutely critical, it's the scarcest resource we've got, right? The few moments that we've been talking now, or that I've been talking now, are a few moments closer to death and it's time I won't ever get back, so I think it's incumbent on us all to think about how we use that time and just re-orientate some of it away from things that we're finding painful and pointless. And spend a bit more time, you know, with things that we find pleasurable and purposeful which would include spending more time with people that we like being with; would include spending a bit more time outdoors, maybe listening to music, all of these things, I think most of us know if we stop and think for a moment, would make us feel a bit happier. The interesting question is why we don't do more of it? And helping others, too, makes us feel nice, too. So all these things that we would get good feedback for if we paid attention to those experiences, but one of the reasons why we don't do those things more is we don't pay attention to those experiences as much as we might, we tell ourselves big stories about the things that we think should make us happy, buying more stuff, earning more money, the kind of narratives and stories that we tell ourselves or we're told by other people that sometimes deviate us off the path of using our time in those ways that make us happier. […] But I think the important thing is that all of us could be a little bit happier by doing some more of the things that make us feel good. And the critical thing is to design environments that make it easier for us to do those things. You know, if you've got a friend that you want to speak to, plan a time in the diary that you speak to them, the same time every week, and then habits will get formed and automatically you speak to that person without having to think too hard about doing so. So, all of us, wherever we start from, I think, can nudge ourselves a little bit happier.

Paul Dolan / Lee Millam: Pod Academy, 5 October 2014. http://podacademy.org/podcasts/happiness-design/

TIPP

In this kind of task you need note-taking skills. First read the tasks carefully in order to know what to listen for and note down. As the information is often given very fast or without further explanation, try not to write down too much but work with graphics, symbols, or pictures. Instead of writing "spending time" you can draw a little clock, and "feeling nice" could be a smiley. This is often faster and more effective. Additionally, do not take notes in German. In the end, it is essential that you write down the information in correct and understandable English. Keep in mind that the tasks follow the chronological order of the listening text.

- **Zu 1:** You only need to concentrate on what Prof. Dolan says: "But some kind of balance between things that we find fun on the one hand and things that we find fulfilling on the other." (ll. 6 f.)
- **Zu 2:** The tricky part here is that client 1 takes some time to say what exactly happiness is for him. Don't let that distract you and stay focused.
"[…] happiness for me […] it's spending time with the people I want to be with, it's not just living from moment to moment but actually just being in the moment and doing the things that are actually most important." (ll. 16 ff.)

- **Zu 3:** Here there are more things mentioned than are needed. The problem lies in taking notes fast enough, so do not forget to use pictures, symbols or abbreviations (e. g. fr+fam for "friends and family"). After listening you should write down the solution in whole words.
  "[…] spending time with my friends and family, going out for dinner, going to watch my football team play football, playing with my cat." (ll. 29 ff.)
- **Zu 4:** Again, more examples are stated than asked for. Focus on two of them:
  "[…] I think it's incumbent on us all to think about how we use that time […] which would include spending more time with people that we like being with; would include spending a bit more time outdoors, maybe listening to music […] And helping others, too, makes us feel nice, too." (ll. 35 ff.)
- **Zu 5:** The difficult thing here is to summarise the content in simpler words. It is fine to just give a short description of what Prof. Dolan said:
  "The interesting question is why we don't do more of it? And helping others, too, <u>makes us feel nice</u>, too. So, all these <u>things that we would get good feedback for</u> if we paid attention to those experiences, but one of the reasons why we don't do those things more is <u>we don't pay attention to those experiences as much as we might</u> […]" (ll. 41 ff.)
- **Zu 6:** Here, the recommendation asked for is introduced by "the important/the critical thing is …":
  "But I think the important thing is that all of us could be a little bit happier by doing some more of the things that make us feel good. And <u>the critical thing is to design environments that make it easier for us to do those things</u>." (ll. 49 ff.)

1
- fun/pleasure (on the one hand)
- things that are fulfilling/purposeful (on the other hand)

2
- being in the moment/spending time with the people you want to be with
- doing things that are most important

3 *(any three out of the following:)* spending time with friends and family, going out for dinner, watching a football match, playing with her cat

4 *(any two out of the following:)* spending time on things we find pleasurable and purposeful, spending time with people we like being with, spending time outdoors, listening to music, helping others

5 We don't pay attention to experiences that we get good feedback for or that would make us feel nice.

6 design environments that make it easier for us to do things that make us feel good

Hörverstehen • Übungsaufgabe 4
Baden-Württemberg • Berufliches Gymnasium • Englisch

Journalism and its audiences

Tess Woodcraft and Prof. Angela Phillips are talking about changes in journalism. While listening, tick (✓) the correct answer (a, b, c or d). There is only one correct answer.

1 Prof. Phillips based her findings on …
   a ☐ news reports.
   b ☐ a scientific book.
   c ☐ young audiences worldwide.

2 The Internet …
   a ☐ has made journalism superfluous.
   b ☐ has changed the way news is consumed and produced.
   c ☐ was seen quite critical by a lot of people at the turn of the century.

3 The "prosumer"-revolution has …
   a ☐ not turned out the way some people expected.
   b ☐ only become reality for technology enthusiasts.
   c ☐ completely changed the way news is produced.

4 Journalists and their audiences …
   a ☐ still do not really work together.
   b ☐ work together now on social media.
   c ☐ do not get into contact with each other.

5 One of the changes for journalism nowadays is that …
   a ☐ everybody can become a quality journalist.
   b ☐ there are more sources available to work with.
   c ☐ the power of journalists is deteriorating significantly.

Lösungen

Transcript — Journalism and its audiences

Tess Woodcraft (reporter): Hello, this is Pod Academy, and I am Tess Woodcraft. Journalism and how we interact with it is changing but what exactly are those changes, and do they matter? I caught up with Professor Angela Phillips, author of Journalism in Context, just before she was due to speak at the […] Future of Journalism conference in Cardiff.

Professor Phillips: I'm interested in the way in which news journalism is changing, and, in particular, how news audiences are changing in relation to changes in the industry. So, I've looked at audiences in my book, *Journalism in Context*, but I've also been looking at young audiences … young news audiences in an international context to see how young people are accessing news.

Tess Woodcraft: So, what's been happening with journalism?

Professor Phillips: Since the rise of the Internet, there have been big changes, not only in how news journalism is produced, but also in how it is consumed. And, these two things are, kind of, in lockstep. At the end of the last century, the beginning of this one, there were a lot of people who were very enthusiastic about the kind of changes. They saw the Internet as being a means of democratising news. They saw audiences being much more involved in news production and they talked about journalists becoming less elitist, more involved in their audiences, and that journalism would become much more of a collaborative process.

Tess Woodcraft: To a certain extent that's happened, hasn't it? We see, for example, the Shoreham Airshow – ordinary people's videos of the crash.

Professor Phillips: In very marginal ways this "prosumer" revolution – the idea of the consumer that also produces – has come to pass, but not in anything like the way in which those web enthusiasts imagined it would. What we have today is people – bystanders with cameras. So, whereas before journalists would have gone and interviewed people about what they saw and it would have been sort of secondary – second-hand information – now if there is a big event like an air crash, like a bombing, there will always be people in the vicinity who have camera phones and will very often put that information into social media where journalists can access it. But actually, this doesn't make them journalists, they are still sources. And although that information moves around – might make it on Twitter or on Facebook or on YouTube – most of what happens is that it is curated by journalists who bring it together and construct a narrative around the information and then repackage it in a different place and a different way. So, although one can look … so, really it is not collaborative. What we're seeing is journalists who in many ways have more power than they used to have – they have the power to find their way into places where they would never, never otherwise have managed to be. The likelihood of a journalist being in the right place at the right time when a bomb goes off are [sic] miniscule. So, the difference we have is that we now have access – to pictures in particular

40 – that we didn't have access to before, but that doesn't really fundamentally change the job of journalists or the relationship between journalist and audience in any way.

Tess Woodcraft/Angela Phillips, Pod Academy, 8 September 2015. http://podacademy.org/podcasts/journalism-and-its-audiences/

TIPP

Watch out for key words given in the task and mark them before the first listening.

- **Zu 1:** Here, the key words are "based her findings on". Prof. Phillips mentions her book, which contains her findings, but they are based on audiences – and specifically "young audiences … young news audiences": "So I've looked at audiences in my book, *Journalism in Context*, but I've also been looking at young audiences … young news audiences in an international context to see how young people are accessing news." (ll. 8 ff.)

- **Zu 2:** Look out for the key words that are underlined here: "Since the rise of the Internet, there have been big <u>changes</u>, not only in how news journalism is <u>produced</u>, but also in how it is <u>consumed</u>." (ll. 12 f.)

- **Zu 3:** The following passage from the text shows that the "prosumer revolution" has not turned out the way "some people" (here: "web enthusiasts") thought it would turn out: "<u>In very marginal ways</u> this 'prosumer' revolution – the idea of the consumer that also produces – has come to pass, but <u>not in anything like the way in which those web enthusiasts imagined</u> it would." (ll. 22 ff.)

- **Zu 4:** Here you need to know that "to collaborate" means "to work together" and that this is not the case here: "… most of what happens is that it is curated by journalists who bring it together and construct a narrative around the information and then repackage it in a different place and a different way […] so, really <u>it is not collaborative</u>. (ll. 32 ff.)

- **Zu 5:** Try to listen for key words such as "sources" and "journalist". Philips talks about "bystanders with cameras" (l. 25) and "information [moving] around" (l. 31), which is not journalism. The statement that journalists are getting less important is also not correct because Phillips explicitly states that "we're seeing […] journalists who in many ways <u>have more power than they used to have</u>" (ll. 35 f.). That leads to the second statement being the correct one: "[…] there will always be people in the vicinity who have camera phones and will very often <u>put that information into social media where journalists can access it</u>." (ll. 28 f.); "So the difference we have is that <u>we now have access – to pictures in particular</u> – that we didn't have access to before […]" (ll. 39 f.)

1. Prof. Phillips based her findings on …
   c ☑ young audiences worldwide.

2. The Internet …
   b ☑ has changed the way news is consumed and produced.

3. The "prosumer"-revolution has …
   a ☑ not turned out the way some people expected.

4. Journalists and their audiences …
   a ☑ still do not really work together.

5. One of the changes for journalism nowadays is that …
   b ☑ there are more sources available to work with.

Hörverstehen · Übungsaufgabe 5

Baden-Württemberg · Berufliches Gymnasium · Englisch

Protecting the climate

Listen to six people talking about climate change. Match each speaker (1 to 6) with one of the opinions (A to G) by putting the corresponding letter into the correct box. For each speaker there is only one correct answer. There is one more opinion than you need.

The speaker ...

A believes that higher costs would make people change their habits concerning behaviour that is damaging to the environment.

B says politics will adopt measures to deal with the problem of climate change.

C is pointing the finger at individuals who refuse to bear responsibility for their actions.

D blames older generations and their blindness with regard to the future.

E wants politicians to take action but does not think the measures they take are sufficient.

F believes that everybody can do something to live a sustainable life.

G questions the impact an individual has and is against restricting people's freedom.

Speaker	1	2	3	4	5	6
Opinion						

Lösungen

Transcript — Protecting the climate

Speaker 1
For my generation – I'm 17 – climate change is a big issue. My friends and I have been to several demonstrations against man-made global warming. Politicians and lawmakers finally need a wake-up call to do more to protect the climate now. I mean, the older generations have lived at our expense! What about the future of the younger generations? We want to live on a planet that's still worth living in! I do hope we can make a difference and manage to change course.

Speaker 2
It worries me to see that the climate is changing at such a fast pace! In my opinion, individuals can do a great deal to contribute to protecting the climate and emitting less CO_2, for example. I live in the city with my family – I'm a mother of two – so it's easy to do without a car – even with two little children. We use public transport, and when we go on holiday we take the train. You'd be surprised how far you can get by railway in Europe – and it can be much more comfortable than flying! We've also met a lot of lovely people on our train journeys – we're still in touch with some of them!

Speaker 3
I'm from the countryside and public transport there is dreadful. So I definitely need my car to get around. I don't know whether you can make a difference as an individual – it's the politicians who have to act. I asked the MP for my constituency to speak up for a regular bus connection to the nearest city, but nothing has been done. There's always a lack of funds. If the government increased its expenditure on rural infrastructure, the number of people who left their car in the garage would rise. That's for sure!

Speaker 4
In my opinion, both individuals and politicians need to act to slow or stop global warming. I only vote for parties that take global warming seriously and support legislation that gives incentives for environmentally friendly behaviour. And why isn't there a tax on jet fuel? If flying got more expensive, maybe fewer people would fly? I, for one, try to fly as little as possible – and what I also do is eat less meat. You know that the methane gas cattle emit contributes a great deal to global warming?

Speaker 5
I don't agree. What difference does it make if some people, say, avoid flying? Other people will take their places. And why should we cut back on our lifestyle? Don't I have the right to fly to Bali in winter when the weather is dreadful here? I can afford it and I just do it. Wouldn't it be unfair to less affluent people if the price of flying increased? They also have the right to fly to Majorca for their summer holidays, for example. And, by the way, if I feel like it, I also treat myself to a juicy steak. I can't make a difference anyway.

Speaker 6
I'm an MP from the south of England. I really understand that an increasing number of citizens are getting more and more impatient with politics as far as global warming is concerned. But I can assure people who are worried that the topic is high on my party's agenda. I know the legislative process can be lengthy and that compromises have to be made, but we're working hard on a ground-breaking legislative package. Both lawmakers and citizens should do their very best to tackle the pressing issue of global warming, however.

> **TIPP**
>
> Here you need to understand the general information or gist of a text. Focus on key words but always pay attention to the context.
>
> - **zu Speaker 1 – D:** "I mean, the older generations have lived at our expense! What about the future of the younger generations?" (ll. 3 ff.) The speaker is pointing a finger at others, which could hint at sentence C. However, she is clearly criticising the older generations as a whole.
>
> - **zu Speaker 2 – F:** "In my opinion, individuals can do a great deal to contribute to protecting the climate and emitting less CO_2, for example." (ll. 7 ff.) You might be tempted to choose C because of "individuals". The speaker, however, gives examples which show that she believes everybody can do something.
>
> - **zu Speaker 3 – E:** "[…] it's the politicians who have to act. […] There's always a lack of funds. If the government increased its expenditure on rural infrastructure the number of people who leave their car in the garage would rise."
> (ll. 16 ff.) The speaker clearly criticises politicians for not doing enough, pointing out what should be done by politics.
>
> - **zu Speaker 4 – A:** "And why isn't there a tax on jet fuel? If flying got more expensive, maybe fewer people would fly?" (ll. 23 f.) The words "tax" and "more expensive" can be seen as a synonym of "higher costs" in the statement. You should not forget to pay attention to different expressions that mean the same.
>
> - **zu Speaker 5 – G:** "What difference does it make if some people, say, avoid flying? Other people will take their places. And why should we cut back on our lifestyle?" (ll. 27 f.) These questions are meant in a rhetorical way and may be distracting, but clearly show the speaker's attitude.
>
> - **zu Speaker 6 – B:** "But I can assure people who are worried that the topic is high on my party's agenda. […] we're working hard on a ground-breaking legislative package." (ll. 36 ff.) The speaker is a politician (l. 34: "MP from the south of England", l. 36 f.: "my party"). "Legislative package" is a synonym for "measures", which are mentioned in the correct statement.

Speaker	1	2	3	4	5	6
Opinion	D	F	E	A	G	B

Robotics

Listen to the following podcast on the topic of robotics. While listening, tick (✓) the correct answer (a, b, c or d). There is only one correct answer.

1 For Alan Winfield, intelligent robotics …
   a ☐ are the type of robots used to make cars.
   b ☐ is different from what we call "autonomous".
   c ☐ can make their own decisions.

2 Autonomous robots …
   a ☐ are only toys.
   b ☐ can be used as household helpers.
   c ☐ are not for individual use at home.

3 Toy robots can be more advanced because …
   a ☐ there are less severe consequences in case of failure.
   b ☐ they are only a test run for more advanced appliances.
   c ☐ they are small enough to test new technologies.

4 One main issue with robotics research today is …
   a ☐ making it safe for children.
   b ☐ finding out how to improve security.
   c ☐ likely to be solved within the next few years.

5 Adam Afriyie is pensive about …
   a ☐ whether robots will act ethically or not.
   b ☐ how much human interaction robots still need.
   c ☐ the scope of allowing robots to make decisions.

6 Mr Afriyie thinks that we require …
   a ☐ official manuals for robots.
   b ☐ legislation concerning robotics.
   c ☐ better computer design.

Lösungen

Transcript — Robotics

Alan Winfield: The new kind of robotics that really has not yet made a big impact in society but is on the verge, if you like … on the cusp of making a big impact is called intelligent robotics. So, intelligent robots unlike those old kind of robots that make cars. Intelligent robots are capable of deciding what to do next on their own. The word that we use is "autonomous". So, the … if you like, the autonomous robot industry is new. The best examples of autonomous robots are really, so far, are toys. So, for instance, you know the Sony Aibo, which was the pet robot dog – that was a very good example of an autonomous mobile robot. Of course, I've forgotten the biggest application of autonomous mobile robots, which is, of course, robot vacuum cleaners. Most of those robots that I've just described are not learning. The toy robots do have some learning functions. One of the reasons, of course, the toy robots can be more advanced is because the scope for things going wrong is smaller. In other words, the potential for it to do harm if it does the wrong thing is much smaller than if it's a robot that's driving your car, for instance. So, typically, we find that the more serious and safety-critical the application, then the less the intelligence or the learning. One of the big challenges that we face in the robotics research community is how to figure out how to make intelligence safe; and that's a problem that we haven't yet cracked. We're just beginning to solve that problem but my guess is it'll be another 10 or 20 years before we can really build intelligent robots that we can have good confidence … are both going to do the right thing and equally importantly, not do the wrong thing.

Chandy Nath: Alan Winfield pointed out that the autonomous robots we have today aren't really that bright. So, toy robot dogs, robot vacuum cleaners – but hopefully the technologies demonstrated at the reception which Lord Salisbury just referred to were at the forefront of current research. Now, we've heard how Lord Salisbury was particularly impressed by the robot arm; Adam Afriyie, was there anything at the reception that particularly caught your eye?

Adam Afriyie: What struck me most was actually – and what Alan raises there – which actually was the ethical debate around how far does one allow robots, these new technologies to make decisions? And one of the speakers pointed out that if, for example, you've got assistive living technologies and an iPad, for example, where an older person who needs some support – maybe they've got Alzheimer's … needs some reminders, needs some medical input – how far do we allow that to go before we say … actually people need human interaction. Now I'll pick one example which is actually that, in the computer industry, computer chips actually design the next generation of computer chips. And, in fact, most technologists will admit they actually don't know how these computer chips work anymore because the … other computers have designed them. So, we're already into this vein where actually we may require those laws of robotics that Asimov first came up with to be applied. […]

Chandy Nath, Parliamentary Recording Unit. http://www.parliament.uk/about/podcasts/scienceinparliament/robotics/

TIPP

In this task you need to listen for detail and also infer the message from the text. It is important that you first read the tasks and alternatives carefully in order to find the correct solution while listening to the text. Many aspects are repeated once or sometimes twice in other words or with examples. This will also help you when parts of the text are mumbled or maybe spoken too fast. So listen closely in order to understand what is said.

- **Zu 1:** "[…] intelligent robots unlike those old kind of robots that make cars. Intelligent robots are capable of <u>deciding what to do next on their own</u>." (ll. 3 f.) "Decide" and "make … decisions" have the same meaning. The phrases "on their own" and "their own decisions" also give you a hint.

- **Zu 2:** "The best examples of autonomous robots are really, so far, are toys. So, for instance, […] the Sony Aibo, which was the pet robot dog – that was a very good example of an autonomous mobile robot. […] <u>the biggest application of autonomous mobile robots, which is, of course, robot vacuum cleaners</u>." (ll. 6 ff.)
The alternative "[…] are only toys" cannot be correct because the speaker talks about different ways of using robots. Toys are just an example. Listen closely and concentrate on the "biggest application", which is "robot vacuum cleaners". This serves as an example of "household helpers".

- **Zu 3:** "One of the reasons, of course, the toy robots can be more advanced is because <u>the scope for things going wrong is smaller</u>." (ll. 11 f.)
The other alternatives use buzz words to distract you. So listen closely to "things going wrong" ("failure"), which gives you the necessary hint. Moreover, it is repeated in the next sentence: "[…] the <u>potential for it to do harm if it does the wrong thing is much smaller</u> than if it's a robot that's driving your car […]" (ll. 13 f.)

- **Zu 4:** "One of the big challenges that we face in the robotics research community is how to figure out <u>how to make intelligence safe</u>; and that's a problem that we haven't yet cracked." (ll. 16 ff.)
The task is about "one main issue", so focus on "the big challenges that we face". The task is not about all the other issues mentioned, only the most important one.

- **Zu 5:** "What struck me most was actually [...] the ethical debate around <u>how far does one allow robots</u>, these new technologies <u>to make decisions</u>?" (ll. 28 ff.)
  The expression "ethical debate" is a distractor here, so listen closely and do not jump to the supposedly obvious solution ("act ethically"). Instead, focus on what is actually said, i. e. how far one allows robots to make decisions.
- **Zu 6:** "So, we're already into this vein where actually we may require those <u>laws of robotics</u> that Asimov first came up with to be applied." (l. 38 f.)
  You do not need to know Asimov's laws to find the correct solution. You should, however, notice the synonymous use of "laws" and "legislation".

1 For Alan Winfield, intelligent robotics …

   c ☑ can make their own decisions.

2 Autonomous robots …

   b ☑ can be used as household helpers.

3 Toy robots can be more advanced because …

   a ☑ there are less severe consequences in case of failure.

4 One main issue with robotics research today is …

   b ☑ finding out how to improve security.

5 Adam Afriyie is pensive about …

   c ☑ the scope of allowing robots to make decisions.

6 Mr Afriyie thinks that we require …

   b ☑ legislation concerning robotics.

Hörverstehen · Übungsaufgabe 7
Baden-Württemberg · Berufliches Gymnasium · Englisch

Brooklyn film school located in working film lot

Listen to the following podcast about the Barry Feirstein Graduate School of Cinema. While listening, complete the notes on the points listed on this worksheet. You do not need to write in complete sentences.

1. What is special about the school: (Name two examples)
   - _____
   - _____

2. Why the school was fortunate: (Name two aspects)
   - _____
   - _____

3. New York City gave around $7 million for …
   - _____
   - _____

4. Why did the city of New York give this sum to the school?
   _____
   _____

5. How the school encourages diversity:
   - _____
   - _____

6. Examples of what the students like at the school:
   - _____
   - _____

Lösungen

Transcript — Brooklyn film school located in working film lot

Reporter: The Steiner Studio lot is home to the brand new Barry Feirstein Graduate School of Cinema, part of the city university system. It is the only film school in New York that's on a film lot. Unlike other prestigious film schools, the Feirstein school is public and costs a third of the price of a private film school. The instructors are all professionals.

Jonathan Wacks *(director of Feirstein):* We had the good fortune to be able to build this from the ground up. So the whole building is brand new, the facility was purpose-built for a film school, and all the equipment is brand new, the students are brand new, the faculty, the whole thing was very, very carefully and consciously designed to be a 21st-century film school.

Reporter: New York City contributed about $7 million for construction and scholarships. City officials say the goal is for a world class school that reflects New York's population.

Luis Castro *(NYC acting commissioner for Media and Entertainment):* If you take a look at their student body, right now about half of the students are women. This first incoming class, about 45 % are from under-represented backgrounds. So, it's a real testament to the school's commitment to helping diversify the industry.

Reporter: Professor Sarah Cawly praises the students' drive and enthusiasm.

Sarah Cawly: I'm not having to whip them up at all. I'm having to guide them and to train them to professional procedures but they're already bringing a lot of enthusiasm to the task.

Ryan Emanuel *(student):* My goal is to be a cinematographer. And the reason why I came here, to Feirstein, is to get a very well-rounded education on how to work both in independent productions and also studio productions.

Rose Haas *(student):* I was working in theatre a lot before I came here. And I really liked … I really like just being in the room with actors and helping create a performance.

Reporter: With the school on the lot, the students are surrounded by professionals making movies.

Jonathan Wacks *(director of Feirstein):* The whole place has got, you know, is packed with trucks and professionals and people going about their business making movies. It creates a, I think, a fantastic atmosphere in which to study film.

Reporter: Doug Steiner, who helped bring the school to his production line, is now looking forward to next year when he hopes to add a media programme from Pittsburgh's Carnegie Mellon University. Bernard Shusman, VOA News, Steiner Studio, Brooklyn, New York.

Bernard Shusman, "Brooklyn Film School Located in Working Film Lot". In: Voice of America News, 6 November 2015.

TIPP

Here you need note-taking skills. First read the tasks carefully in order to know what to listen for and note down. As the information is often given fast or without further explanation, try not to write down too much but work with graphics, symbols, or pictures. This is often faster and more effective. Additionally, do not take notes in German. In the end, it is essential that you write down the information in correct and understandable English.

- **Zu 1:** "It is the only film school in New York that's on a film lot. Unlike other prestigious film schools, the Feirstein school is public and costs a third of the price of a private film school." (ll. 2 ff.)
  Two expressions will give you a hint here: "the only film school", "unlike other". They will help you figure out the correct two aspects. Moreover, there is a third aspect ("costs a third of the price of a private film school") in case you overheard one of the others.

- **Zu 2:** "We had the good fortune to be able to build this from the ground up. So the whole building is brand new, the facility was purpose-built for a film school, and all the equipment is brand new, the students are brand new, the faculty, the whole thing was very, very carefully and consciously designed to be a 21st-century film school." (ll. 6 ff.)
  There are several aspects mentioned after "We had the good fortune to […]". Focus on two of them to write them down correctly.

- **Zu 3:** "New York City contributed about $7 million for construction and scholarships." (ll. 11 f.)

- **Zu 4:** Right after the sum is mentioned you get to know why the money was given: "City officials say the goal is for a world class school that reflects New York's population." (ll. 12 f.)

- **Zu 5:** "[…] right now about half of the students are women. This first incoming class, about 45 % are from under-represented backgrounds. So, it's a real testament to the school's commitment to helping diversify the industry." (ll. 15 ff.)
  The key words here are "diversity" in the task and "diversify" in the text.

- **Zu 6:** "And the reason why I came here, to Feirstein, is to get a very well-rounded education on how to work both in independent productions and also studio productions." (ll. 22 ff.), "I really like just being in the room with actors and helping create a performance." (l. 26)
  Listen closely to the different speakers and you might find out who is a student and who is not. This will help you get examples of what students like at the school, introduced by phrases like "the reason why I came here" or "I really like".

1
- it is on a film lot / on the premises of a film lot
- it is public / it costs much less than private schools

2
- facility purpose-built (for a film school) / specifically designed to be a film school
- brand new building and equipment / everything brand new (building, equipment, students, teachers)

3
- construction
- scholarships

4 (the goal is) to have a world class school (reflecting the city's population)

5
- half of the students are female/women
- 45 % / many students from under-represented backgrounds / from minorities

6
- well-rounded education (work on independent as well as studio productions)
- being together with actors

Hörverstehen · Übungsaufgabe 8
Baden-Württemberg · Berufliches Gymnasium · Englisch

Most adolescents do not exercise enough to stay healthy

Listen to a podcast which deals with a survey about teenagers' physical activity. While listening, tick (✓) the correct answer (a, b, c or d). There is only one correct answer.

1. The WHO study says that …
   a ☐ in 142 of 146 countries boys were more physically active than girls.
   b ☐ 11- to 17-year-olds in the USA and Ireland are least physically active.
   c ☐ 1.6 million young people aged 11 to 17 are not physically active enough.

2. If you do regular physical exercise at a young age you …
   a ☐ will be more likely to be active as an adult.
   b ☐ get benefits from your health insurance company.
   c ☐ won't have to exercise so much anymore when you are an adult.

3. Ms Guthold says that …
   a ☐ young people should play more.
   b ☐ young people should do 20 minutes of exercise a day.
   c ☐ it is not important what kind of daily exercise you do to stay fit.

4. The study does not say that physical workouts have an effect on …
   a ☐ social skills.
   b ☐ intellectual abilities.
   c ☐ emotional intelligence.

5. Ms Riley says one of the reasons for the high level of inactivity is …
   a ☐ bad nutrition.
   b ☐ too many cars.
   c ☐ electronic and digital progress.

6. According to the WHO, one way out of this situation would be …
   a ☐ free bicycles for young people.
   b ☐ more and different kinds of sport at school.
   c ☐ more parks in the cities for young people to meet.

Lösungen

Transcript — Most adolescents do not exercise enough to stay healthy

A report finds most adolescents around the world do not get enough physical activity on a daily basis to be healthy and to stay healthy as adults. This World Health Organization study presents the first-ever global estimates of insufficient physical activity among adolescents ages 11 to 17. Data for this study was collected from 1.6 million adolescents across 146 countries. It finds girls were less active than boys in all but four countries – Tonga, Samoa, Afghanistan and Zambia. The report says the biggest gender gaps are seen in the United States and Ireland where 15 percent more girls than boys were physically inactive. The World Health Organization recommends adolescents do moderate or vigorous exercises for one hour every day of the week to stay fit. Regina Guthold is a scientist in the WHO's Department of Maternal, Newborn, Child and Adolescent Health, and lead author of the study. She says the 60-minute workouts can be split into three segments of 20 minutes a day for health benefits to kick in. She also points out that adolescents get better heart health and that they have better respiratory fitness. They have better cognitive function too – easier learning – and they have better pro-social behavior. And, it is likely that the benefits track into adulthood, meaning that active adolescents are likely to be active adults and then they get the health benefits as adults as well. Guthold says any kind of physical activity is good. This could include walking or biking to school, team sports, dancing, active domestic chores, physical education and planned exercise. The study finds young people everywhere in the world do not exercise enough. Data shows that 85 percent of girls and 78 percent of boys do not meet the current WHO recommendations of at least one hour of physical activity a day. The co-author of the study, Leanne Riley, cites some of the causes behind this high level of inactivity. She says we have had this electronic revolution that seems to have changed adolescents' movement patterns and encourages them to sit more, to be less active, to drive more, walk less, be less active in general and then be more involved in digital play rather than active play. The WHO says schools should encourage physical education and get students to be more active in competitive and non-competitive sports. It recommends city and community leaders should create paths for young people to walk and cycle safely and independently. It says urban planning also has a big role to play in designing safer recreational play areas in parks for young people.

Lisa Schlein, "Most Adolescents Do Not Exercise Enough to Stay Healthy, Study Finds". In: Voice of America News, 12 November 2019

TIPP

Watch out for key words given in the task and mark them before the first listening.

- **Zu 1:** Do not be confused by the various numbers given in the task and the text. Look out for what is said about boys and girls regarding physical fitness. As in only four of 146 countries girls were more active, there are 142 countries left in which it is the other way round: "Data for this study was collected from 1.6 million adolescents <u>across 146 countries. It finds girls were less active than boys in all but four countries</u> – Tonga, Samoa, Afghanistan and Zambia." (ll. 4 ff.)

- **Zu 2:** Here, the word "benefits" does not refer to health insurance but indicates that people who are active when young will also be healthy later in life: "And, it is likely that the benefits track into adulthood, meaning that <u>active adolescents are likely to be active adults and then they get the health benefits as adults</u> as well." (ll. 15 ff.)

- **Zu 3:** "Guthold says <u>any kind of physical activity is good</u>. This could include walking or biking to school, team sports, dancing, active domestic chores, physical education and planned exercise." (ll. 17 ff.)
 From the findings of the study you can easily infer that physical exercise is important for adolescents, no matter what kind of activity it is. You could also conclude from the text that young people should play more, but this is not specific enough (e. g. team sports?) and not explicitly mentioned. It is also not said that the gender gap is too small to be paid attention to.

- **Zu 4:** "[…] they have <u>better respiratory fitness</u>. They have <u>better cognitive function</u> too – easier learning – and they have <u>better pro-social behavior</u>." (ll. 13 ff.)
 The task requires an aspect that is not mentioned in connection with physical workouts. Listen closely, as the aspects that are relevant are described with different words in the text: "intellectual abilities" = "cognitive function", "pro-social behavior" = "social skills".

- **Zu 5:** In the text, only the negative effects of electronic and digital progress are mentioned: "[…] Leanne Riley, cites some of the causes behind this high level of inactivity. She says <u>we have had this electronic revolution that seems to have changed adolescents' movement patterns</u> and encourages them to sit more, to be less active, to drive more, walk less, be less active in general and then be <u>more involved in digital play</u> rather than active play." (ll. 22 ff.)

- **Zu 6:** The text only says that the WHO suggests "[…] <u>schools should encourage physical education</u> and get students to be more active <u>in competitive and non-competitive sports</u>." (ll. 26 ff.) Free bicycles and more parks are not mentioned.

1. The WHO study says that …
   a ☑ in 142 of 146 countries boys were more physically active than girls.

2. If you do regular physical exercise at a young age you …
   a ☑ will be more likely to be active as an adult.

3. Ms Guthold says that …
   c ☑ it is not important what kind of daily exercise you do to stay fit.

4. The study does not say that physical workouts have an effect on …
   c ☑ emotional intelligence.

5. Ms Riley says one of the reasons for the high level of inactivity is …
   c ☑ electronic and digital progress.

6. According to the WHO, one way out of this situation would be …
   b ☑ more and different kinds of sport at school.

Lesen und Schreiben · Übungsaufgabe 1
Baden-Württemberg · Berufliches Gymnasium · Englisch

Aufgabe 1: Integrierte Aufgabe zum Leseverstehen

Outline the problems women in politics are faced with according to the author as well as the solutions she presents.

Aufgabe 2: Textanalyse

Analyse the means and strategies the author employs in order to convey her attitude towards Jacinda Ardern's resignation.

Aufgabe 3: Erörterung / Stellungnahme

3.1 Textbezogen und materialbezogen

Comment on the author's statement "No wonder Jacinda's knackered" (ll. 58/59), also taking into account the message of the cartoon.

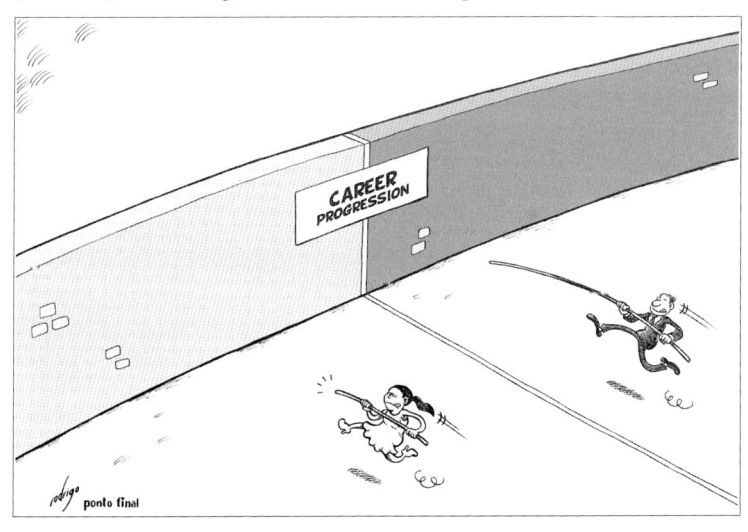

Rodrigo de Matas / Cartoon Movement

3.2 Themenbezogen

One year after your exams you are asked by your school to give the graduation speech for the next graduates. Write the script for your speech assessing the chances and challenges young people face in the 21st century. Put a special focus on gender imbalances.

| Text | Jess Phillips[1], "Women suffer guilt, abuse and disapproval. No wonder Jacinda Ardern[2] is knackered"

Jacinda Ardern has no gas left in the tank to continue as the prime minister of New Zealand. Her resignation speech was the sort of rare and dignified moment that we have come to expect from her, as a woman who presented the world with the kind of leadership that uniquely leant on her emotional intelligence. I'll miss her tone and grace. She leaves a legacy she can be proud of.

I have been thinking about what burned the fuel that she relied on to govern.

Firstly I have no doubt that she felt the constant guilt that pretty much every woman in the world feels the moment they evacuate their womb of a child. Even the Mary Poppins[3]-style perfect, Instagram-polished mothers of the world fret that something they do will harm their child in some way. I asked my husband, who has always been our son's primary carer, if he ever felt guilty for missing a school play or staying late at work. He looked at me baffled; the concept was lost on him. He just thinks, "I had to go to work," and that's the beginning and end of that moral maze for him. For me, there is a constant torture and self-loathing about how my choices might affect them. No matter how I try to push away the societal grooming, it is always there. For Ardern there will have been column inches aplenty to keep the torture prickling her skin.

This is not to say that most working women don't just push through this: they do so every single day in every single workforce in the country. It just burns up fuel, fuel that others don't need to spend. It is tiring and saps our bandwidth.

The pressure pushed on to working women is tiring enough without it being amped up by being a public woman – and the worst of all offences, to some, a political woman. The thing that burns my fuel to the point of a flashing emergency light and a blaring alarm is the abuse and threat of violence that has become par for the course for political women. Jacinda Ardern will have suffered this mercilessly. Today, colleagues and admirers discussed the extent to which that constant threat of abuse contributed to her burnout.

Those threats came from many sources, too: people who hate progressive women and believe they are damning masculinity; anti-vaxxers[4] outraged by her tough Covid stance; those with a general loathing of all politicians.

Combine the two fuel burners and what you end up with is the terrible guilt, fear and shame that decisions you have made in your career, or your political stances (no matter how much you believe in them), put your children, loved ones and employees in danger.

Moments before I started writing this, I spoke to a woman who works for me who told me she wouldn't be in work on a particular day because she had to give evidence in court after an incident in my office. She was not the target: it was me. When my children at school have to answer questions from their classmates about stances I have taken, or are told hateful and untrue things that have been published about me, or when they act hyper-vigilantly in public crowds, aware of the threat to us, my heart breaks and more fuel burns up.

No doubt this is something all men and women in political life experience. However, studies show that the level of violence – often sexualised violence – and the threat that female politicians face is incomparable. I am used to it. I wish I wasn't; but I also wish I was a size 10. But I will also never get used to the effect it has on other people; it is so very tiring. It's just something else I have to consider on top of worrying about policy and details, and fallout, and loyalties. It burns fuel.

What can we do about it? Like Jacinda, I believe the answer is being honest about the fact that politics is an emotional not a bureaucratic game. And constantly pushing for a more empathetic political environment, which will be brought about by having more female leaders and politicians, not fewer.

I am not so idealistic as to think politics is going to change its stripes in my time. But we must build the structures into our politics and our media that damn and criminalise the perpetrators of this abuse, and those who make massive profits from spreading it. We must create support structures female politicians and activists can lean on without being seen negatively or as weak.

Alas, even as I pen my suggestions for change, I know that it is women who will have to do the labour to achieve it, just like we always do. This work takes more fuel – fuel others don't have to use up in the pursuit of a political life. No wonder Jacinda's knackered. *(825 words)*

Jess Phillips: Women suffer guilt, abuse and disapproval. No wonder Jacinda Ardern is knackered, https://www.theguardian.com/commentisfree/2023/jan/20/women-guilt-abuse-disapproval-jacinda-ardern, Copyright Guardian News & Media Ltd 2023

Wortangaben:

1 Jess Phillips: *1981, British Labour MP since 2015
2 Jacinda Ardern: *1980, Prime Minister of New Zealand from 2017 to 2023, when she voluntarily resigned from her post
3 Mary Poppins: a wonderful nanny with magical skills, the protagonist of a novel series, which was later turned into a musical
4 anti-vaxxer: someone who is sceptical about or opposes vaccination

Lösungen

1 **TIPP**

This assignment requires you to focus on two aspects of the text: the problems women in politics face on the one hand and the proposed solutions for these problems on the other. While reading, you should highlight these aspects and then rephrase them in your own words. Also write a short introduction, in which you name the basic facts about the article you are to summarise.

You could mention the following points:
- problems women in politics face:
  - constant guilt that they are not doing enough for their children (cf. ll. 7–14)
  - societal scrutiny (cf. ll. 15/16)
  - women suffer harassment for being in politics (cf. ll. 22–24)
  - fear that family or co-workers might suffer by proxy (cf. ll. 30–33)
  - exhausting especially for women; men do not experience it at the same level (cf. ll. 10–13, 41–43)
- proposed solutions:
  - changing the perception of politics: significance of emotions (cf. ll. 47/48)
  - working towards a respectful atmosphere in politics by increasing the number of women (cf. ll. 48–50)
  - on a societal level, not only should harassing female public figures be condemned but also its propagation in the media (cf. ll. 52–54)
  - the need for support should not be perceived as a weakness; instead, there should be standard practices to assist people in times of crisis (cf. ll. 54/55)
- conclusion: Phillips warns that these changes will only come about if women take on the extra responsibility to promote them (cf. ll. 56/57)

In her article "Women Suffer Guilt, Abuse and Disapproval. No Wonder Jacinda Ardern Is Knackered", which was published in the Guardian in January 2023, Jess Phillips describes problems women in politics are faced with. She also offers ideas on how to tackle these issues. **introduction**

Her central argument is that the price men and women pay for being politically active is essentially different: While men's involvement is generally accepted, women suffer societal scrutiny or even harassment for dedicating their lives to politics. As a consequence, female politicians have to expend much more mental energy than men because, in addition to their workload, they also fear that their co-workers or family could be made responsible for their political decisions and thus suffer by proxy. Above that, women with children are often made to feel constantly guilty that they are not fulfilling their maternal role in an acceptable way, which is aggravated by **problems** women in politics face media outlets and colleagues pointing fingers when a woman seems to prioritise her political career over her role as a caretaker.

Since many of these problems are rooted in traditional notions of women's role in society, Phillips suggests tackling the issues from a related angle. She proposes changing the perception of politics by accepting that political dealings rely on emotional factors to a great extent. Ultimately, all parties involved should cooperate to reach a more respectful atmosphere in politics. On a societal level, not only should harassing female public figures be condemned, but also its propagation in the media. As a side effect, a person's need for support should not be perceived as a weakness; instead, there should be standard practices to assist people in times of crisis. — **proposed solutions**

In conclusion, Phillips claims that increasing the number of women in politics is a vital prerequisite for accomplishing her aims. So, change will only come if women take on the extra responsibility to promote it even though this will increase their workload even more. — **conclusion**

(322 words)

2 TIPP

This assignment requires you to do two things: first, you have to identify the author's attitude towards Jacinda Ardern and her resignation, and second you have to find the stylistic devices and means of language that she employs to express this attitude. You should not forget to support your arguments by quoting from the text.

When you write your analysis, make sure you use your own words and structure your text in a logical order, e. g. by the strategies employed or by some general ideas expressed by them. Avoid strictly following the structure of the text, or you will run the risk of ending up with a re-narration.

In your analysis, you could start by examining the way the author characterises Jacinda Ardern before going on to analyse the strategies she uses in dealing with her central topic: the exhaustion felt by women in politics.

The sample solution mentions the following points:
- introduction: headline already shows empathy with Jacinda Ardern
- characterisation of Ardern by the use of positive words:
  - "rare and dignified" (l. 2)
  - "uniquely leant on her emotional intelligence" (l. 4)
  - "grace" (l. 5)
  - "legacy she can be proud of" (l. 5)
- personal style to create common ground between herself and Jacinda Ardern:
  - calling her by her first name and using colloquial language ("knackered") (cf. ll. 47, 58/59)
  - frequent use of pronoun "I"

- sharing of personal anecdotes from her own (political) life:
  → conversation between Jess Phillips and her husband, who is "baffled" by her feelings of guilt (cf. ll. 10–14)
  → worries about co-workers and children (cf. ll. 34–40)
- generalisation of the (almost desperate) situation and creating a feeling of togetherness among women:
  - "we"/"our" (cf. ll. 2, 19, 47)
  - "pretty much every woman in the world" (cf. ll. 7/8)
  - sarcastic exaggeration: "Even the Mary Poppins-style perfect, Instagram-polished mothers" (ll. 8/9)
  - repetitions: "working women" (ll. 17, 20), "every single day in every single workforce in the country" (l. 18)
  - "Alas, […], I know that it is women who will have to do the labour to achieve it, just like we always do." (ll. 56/57)
- figurative language and other stylistic devices to convey exhaustion and the double burden on women:
  - "has no gas left in the tank" (l. 1)
  - "fuel" (ll. 6, 18, 22, 40, 46, 57/58)
  - "the torture prickling her skin" (l. 16)
  - "fuel that others don't need to spend" (ll. 18/19), "fuel others don't have to use up" (l. 58)
  - "a flashing emergency light and a blaring alarm" (ll. 22/23)
  - "fuel burners" (l. 30)
  - enumerations: "When my children at school have to answer questions from their classmates about stances I have taken, or are told hateful and untrue things that have been published about me, or when they act hyper-vigilantly in public crowds, aware of the threat to us" (ll. 36–39); "policy and details, and fallout, and loyalties" (l. 46)
- conclusion: article's tone almost resigned and completely understanding of Ardern's decision

---

In her article, Jess Phillips expresses sympathy for Ardern's decision to step down from her post as prime minister of New Zealand. Her understanding already becomes evident in the heading of the article, which both enumerates the issues women in politics have to struggle with and concludes with the empathetic statement, "No Wonder Jacinda Ardern Is Knackered". introduction: **headline**

Phillips strives to engage the same empathy in her readers by describing Jacinda Ardern in very positive words. She praises the ex-prime minister's style of governing as inimitably superior by pointing out her "dignified" (l. 2) manner, her "emotional intelligence" (l. 4) and her "grace" (l. 5) as well as by predicting that Ardern will be able to look back on her time in office with satisfaction (cf. l. 5). By furthermore using the adjective "rare" (l. 2) and the adverb **positive words** to characterise Jacinda Ardern "uniquely" (l. 4), she sets Jacinda Ardern apart from other politicians.

A politically active woman herself, Phillips clearly empathises with the extra workload Ardern had to deal with during her time in office. She emphasises this common ground by referring to Ardern by her first name, for example in line 47 and especially at the end of her article where she repeats the conclusion from the headline, only in an even more colloquial register (cf. ll. 58/59). Other strategies underline Phillips' personal style and support the fact that she can perfectly imagine the burdens Jacinda Ardern had to shoulder. Not only does she use the pronoun "I" repeatedly (cf. ll. 4, 6, 7, 10, 34, 37, 43, 44, 45, 47, 51, 56), but she also shares some anecdotes from her own life with her readers, for example in lines 34 to 40 when she describes a very real threat to herself, her employees and her children.

personal style to create common ground

Her main thesis is that regardless of who the primary carer in the family is, women tend to chastise themselves more than men for not prioritising their children. This thesis is also introduced from a personal viewpoint, making the gender imbalance obvious: She describes a conversation she had with her husband, for whom guilt about not constantly being with his children seems to be a completely foreign feeling (cf. ll. 10–13) in contrast to her own "torture and self-loathing" (l. 14).

example of conversation between Jess Phillips and her husband

From this personal take, she goes on to generalise women's situation: Her feelings of guilt and inadequacy are common for "pretty much every woman in the world" (ll. 7/8), she claims. Even those women, whom Phillips sarcastically calls "Mary Poppins-style perfect, Instagram-polished mothers" (ll. 8/9) will know what she means.

generalisation of women's situation

A statement like this stresses Phillips' point that there seems to be simply no way out of the dilemma "societal grooming" (l. 15) has pushed upon "working women" (ll. 17, 20). The use of repetition underlines the monotony and desperation of their fight against impossible expectations: "every single day in every single workforce in the country" (l. 18).

almost desperate situation

Throughout her text, Phillips also regularly employs the first person plural to create a feeling of togetherness and solidarity among her female readers. Ardern's situation is turned into a shared experience through the use of words like "we" and "our" (cf. ll. 2, 19, 47). A particularly striking example of this strategy can be found in the concluding realisation that it is women like Ardern and Phillips – and probably her readers too – who will have to bear the responsibility of change, "just like we always do" (l. 57).

creating a feeling of togetherness

The exasperation behind this realisation, which is further stressed by the introductory expression "Alas" (l. 56), puts into new focus the main cause for Ardern's resignation, namely her exhaustion from the double burden of her political responsibilities as well as the family role society expects of her. This is reflected in Phillips' choice of words: regardless of whether she refers to her own fatigue or Ardern's, the author's language is highly figurative, playing mainly with the theme of "fuel". Not only does she assume that Ardern "has no gas left in the tank" (l. 1) or reflect on "what burned the fuel that she relied on" (l. 6), she also compares the energy women in politics have to expend to fuel several times (e. g. ll. 18, 22, 40, 46) and the multiple problems they face, like societal scrutiny and outright harassment, to "fuel burners" (l. 30).

figurative language to convey **exhaustion**

She concludes by repeating her argument that it is especially the double standards that affect men and women differently that drive women to exhaustion: Figuratively speaking, women need more fuel than men (cf. ll. 18/19, 57/58). Politics is strenuous anyway, as the enumerations in lines 36 to 39 and line 46 show, but for women the burdens are even heavier. This is further stressed by the use of very drastic metaphorical language, such as the constant "torture" (l. 16) of society's expectations or the "flashing emergency light and […] blaring alarm" (ll. 22/23) that signify the severity of the problem.

double burden on women

In a way, Jess Phillips' article sounds rather resigned. She makes it clear that in the current political and social climate, a decision like Jacinda Ardern's to step down from her post as prime minister is completely understandable and almost unavoidable. Yet, by also clearly expressing her regret about this development (cf. ll. 4/5), Phillips urgently appeals to society for change, even if it might take a long time (cf. l. 51).

conclusion

(897 words)

3.1 TIPP

For this assignment, you are supposed to verbalise your own attitude towards the author's statement as well as to the given cartoon, which supports and also broadens the message of Jess Phillips' text. Accordingly, you should start by making up your mind as to your own position. If you agree with Jess Phillips and the cartoonist, find arguments and examples why. You should also go beyond the text and include your background knowledge to do so. Of course, you could also decide to disagree although finding arguments might be a bit harder in that case, as the article and cartoon already guide you in a certain direction. When it comes to putting forward your opinion, be careful not to ramble but focus on the text and the cartoon respectively and give your opinion in a structured and logical way.

The sample solution mentions the following points:
- introduction: general agreement with Jess Phillips' point of view
- message of Phillips' article summarised:
  - Ardern's exhausting position as one of few female political leaders
  - particularly difficult to juggle society's expectations of a working mother
- description and interpretation of the cartoon:
  - man and woman in pole vaulting competition, where the wall symbolises career progression; man has larger pole than woman
  - message: career progression is made more difficult for women
- arguments which prove the message of the cartoon (and the article) right:
  - employers often more reluctant to hire or promote women
  - pressure on working mothers (both from the inside and the outside)
  - traditional male dominance in the world of business hinders women's career progression
- concluding comment on the message of text and cartoon: disparity of opportunities for men and women
- conclusion: real equality has not been reached yet

In her article for *The Guardian*, Jess Phillips expresses sympathy for Jacinda Ardern's decision to step down from her post as prime minister of New Zealand. According to her, society almost forced her to come to this point of exhaustion, which is an opinion I would agree with.	**introduction**
Throughout her premiership, Ardern was not only faced with the challenges of leading the country, overseeing the government's policies and programmes and managing New Zealand's relations with other countries, but also had to come to terms with being one of the few women on the stage of international politics. According to Phillips, this role constituted an asset as well as an obstacle for Ardern. On the one hand, she claims that Ardern's distinct style of leadership benefited New Zealand's politics by allowing emotions and empathy to play a part in the office of prime minister. On the other hand, Phillips points out that not only Ardern's gender, but also her double roles as politician and mother meant that she had to work twice as hard as her male counterparts to be accepted in her position. This is an observation that many women will be able to confirm.	**message** of Phillips' article
While on the surface our society seems to have achieved gender equality, offering equal educational opportunities to girls and boys alike, once a woman enters the job market, she will hit obstacles unnoticed by her male colleagues. The cartoon illustrates this perfectly: On the surface, both candidates seem to face the same challenge in their career progression, but the woman's chance of overcoming the barrier is hampered by the significantly shorter pole she has. Thus, even though she actually seems slightly ahead (defying	description and interpretation of the **cartoon**

her heels and dress), the man she is competing with will probably take the barrier first, or at least with less effort than her. She is literally going to hit a brick wall in her attempt to rise, and if she ultimately manages to vault over the wall, the effort will have cost her considerably more energy than her male competitor.

In reality, the shorter pole can take many forms – women are held back from rising in their professional life in multiple ways. To start with, employers prefer to hire men because they supposedly are less likely to go on prolonged paternity leave. As a result, the expectation that women might focus less on their careers than on family encumbers their progression from very early on. Working mothers are expected not to work full time, which reduces their opportunities to present themselves for promotion and limits their salary as well as their retirement pay.

<small>**arguments:** employers' reluctance to hire or promote women</small>

You could say that this is a question of priorities and that part-time workers put their offspring before their career voluntarily. Unfortunately, however, even if women do choose a career, they might not be totally happy with their decision because deep inside, many of them will feel a nagging sense of inadequacy, draining them of their energy and preventing them from focusing on their goals as much as men can. This sense is either applied from the outside by a society that still scrutinises women for pursuing their personal goals instead of focusing on care work, or by women themselves because they have subconsciously imbibed these societal values.

<small>pressure on working mothers</small>

Even women who remain childless often encounter a metaphorical glass ceiling in the world of business that prevents them from advancing in their career in the same way their male colleagues do. The reasons for this are very complex, but prejudices as well as tradition and so-called old boys' networks certainly play a role. As long as most positions of power are still filled with men, the indirect or direct discrimination against women will probably continue.

<small>traditional male dominance in the world of business</small>

As a consequence, a majority of women will have experienced inequality in their career progression and especially working mothers will be able to empathise with Jess Phillips' experience when she describes a constant feeling of guilt over neglecting her children and a sense of exhaustion from a double mental load her partner is totally unused to. His plans and ambitions are not hampered by social expectations of his behaviour. Admittedly, there is a growing number of men who try to break out of these stereotypical roles, and many of them suffer the same social backlash as women: they forgo career opportunities and lose pay. But still – to stay in the context of the cartoon – by and large men are allowed to choose the height of the walls and the length of the poles they use to vault themselves. The sky is their limit.

<small>**concluding comment:** disparity of opportunities</small>

Considering these disparities, it is too early to celebrate gender equality because women are still subject to scrutiny concerning their private and professional lives. Multiple women are up against exhaustion every day, and Jacinda Ardern's resignation has finally made this glaringly obvious. Let us hope that this will serve as a wake-up call that our society's double standards need to change – not only in politics, but for all women, in the job force as well as in their roles as carers: No woman is automatically destined to be a mother and housewife first and a career woman second, but the full set of opportunities should be extended to everyone and all duties, professional as well as domestic ones, should be shared equally among the genders. *(884 words)* — conclusion

3.2 TIPP

This creative assignment is more open than 3.1. You are not required to refer to the original text, but of course you may draw on ideas from it as well as on your background knowledge. When it comes to content, make sure you mention both chances and challenges young people in the 21st century face. While you might be tempted to concentrate on the challenges, as they are also the main focus of the article you have read, do not forget the fictional celebratory occasion for which you write your text. You are required to assume the role of a speaker at a graduation ceremony, so you should not only talk about negative things but also praise and encourage your listeners. Also pay attention to the formal requirements of a speech, such as the correct way of addressing your audience or the use of stylistic devices to keep the attention of your listeners. Although a genuine speech would not be put down on paper word for word, you should make sure to write complete sentences and use an appropriate register. Do not forget to wrap your speech up by referring to your listeners' situation again.

The sample solution is structured in the following way:
- address to the audience
- introduction: reference to the situation of the graduation ceremony
- chances in the 21st century
- challenges the graduates face, with a focus on gender imbalance:
  - elaboration on imbalances: female perspective
  - elaboration on imbalances: male perspective
- graduates' chance to change the world for the better
- (humorous) conclusion
- greeting

Dear graduates, — address

I feel honoured to be standing here before you today as you celebrate your graduation. Congratulations to each and every one of you for — introduction: reference to the situation your hard work, dedication and perseverance. This time last year, I was in your place, and I remember the feeling of elation: finally, you can take your lives into your own hands. The future is wide open! So, before you start the next chapter of your lives, I want to take a moment to reflect on the chances and challenges that young people face in the 21st century.

When I look at you, I see a group of young, gifted people impatient to try out their talents and accomplish their dreams. The world is your oyster! And never have young people had more opportunities before them than our generation. We are spoilt for choice. All the same I'd like to warn you – there are still challenges ahead you might not be aware of yet. *(chances in the 21st century)*

True, we worry about climate change, international conflicts, financial crises and our chances on the employment market. But some of the most unexpected challenges you might encounter are the persistent gender imbalances that still exist in our society. Despite the significant progress that has been made in recent years, women continue to face systemic barriers that limit their opportunities and potential. It's no secret that the gender pay gap has still not been overcome, with women earning less than men for the same work in many areas. It is a blatant fact that women are underrepresented in leadership positions across all sectors, from art to business to politics. *(challenges: focus on gender imbalance)*

How is this possible, with more girls than boys graduating from school with top grades? Shouldn't more women reach leading positions? Where do all the highly qualified women go? The simple answer is: More often than not, they go to several places at once and often work harder than their male peers. Apart from pursuing their career, they also carry around the mental as well as physical load of caring for children, friends or elderly parents. That can be highly rewarding on a personal level, but on a professional level, it is exhausting and financially costly. You cannot climb the career ladder as high and as fast as your competitors with a double burden on your back. You cannot progress as far as others if an invisible glass ceiling blocks your way. So, to all the young women before me today: be vigilant. You might have to work twice as hard as the young men sitting next to you to reach the same level of success. *(elaboration on imbalances: female perspective)*

Admittedly, it's not just women who are impacted by gender inequality. Men, too, are affected by rigid gender norms that limit their ability to express themselves and pursue their interests freely, and they might suffer the consequences if they try to break out of traditional male role patterns. So, I think it would be in everybody's best interest if we try and break down ALL the barriers of gender expec- *(male perspective)* tations. After all, what do we have to lose except the unfair advantage of one gender over the other, respectively the suffocating rigidness of conforming to a pre-fixed identity?

Joking aside, ultimately it will be a win for everybody when we reach true equality because only then can we reach our true potential. Despite all the challenges before us, I'm optimistic about the future. "Why?", you may ask. "Why should we be able to change societal patterns that have been entrenched for years?" Let me put it quite simply: because you know so much about various lifestyles these days, you have met so many different people throughout your school career and you have let yourselves feel enriched instead of threatened by their diversity. And last but not least, you have learnt to ask all the critical questions. So, I truly believe that our generation has the chance to create a more equitable and just society, where gender roles no longer limit opportunities and freedom. It starts with each of us, as individuals, challenging our own biases and assumptions about societal norms. As you move forward and leave your school years behind you, I'd like to encourage you to embrace the challenges ahead of you. Never stop asking! Together, you can make the world a better place! *— graduates' chance to change the world for the better*

At the end of my speech, I want to address you girls again: If it sometimes feels as if you have to work twice as hard to achieve your goals as everybody else – in the end, pursuing your dream will be worth the effort. I'd like to conclude with some famous words about the dancer Ginger Rogers: "After all, she did everything that Fred Astaire did. She just did it backwards and in high heels." *— conclusion*

Congratulations again, dear graduates. The world is at your feet, high-heeled or not. *— greeting*

(808 words)

Lesen und Schreiben · Übungsaufgabe 2
Baden-Württemberg · Berufliches Gymnasium · Englisch

Aufgabe 1: Integrierte Aufgabe zum Leseverstehen

Outline the development of segregation since the 1960s. Use your own words.

Aufgabe 2: Textanalyse

Analyse the author's attitude towards the segregation that influences her private life and how her attitude is conveyed.

Aufgabe 3: Erörterung/Stellungnahme

3.1 Textbezogen und materialbezogen

"People [...] who may even have black 'friends' or lovers, still too often manage to have a community that doesn't reflect diversity in their broader city or nation." (ll. 22–25)

Comment on the statement from the text and include the findings of the following statistics.

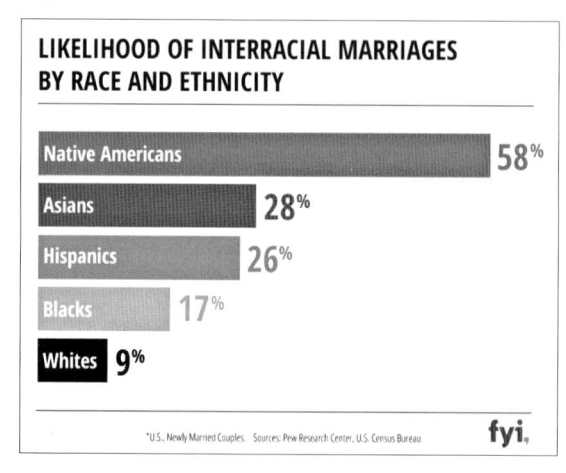

LIKELIHOOD OF INTERRACIAL MARRIAGES BY RACE AND ETHNICITY

Race/Ethnicity	Percentage
Native Americans	58%
Asians	28%
Hispanics	26%
Blacks	17%
Whites	9%

U.S. Newly Married Couples. Sources: Pew Research Center, U.S. Census Bureau

fyi.

© FYI Networks

3.2 Themenbezogen

You read the article below on *The Guardian*'s website. Write an entry for the comment section in which you express your own thoughts as to the current state of segregation in the US and to Allen's opinion about it.

| Text | **Our 21st-Century Segregation: We're Still Divided by Race**

Even now, there are two Americas: one for brown people, one for whites. The difference is that we choose it today.

1   Many Americans don't want to admit it, but I'll say it: segregation is still around. Sometimes by design. And sometimes by choice.

Let me be clear, this isn't the segregation of my parents' era. It's not a legally mandated and enforced system backed by public figures like former Alabama [governor] George Wallace, who famously said, "Segregation today. Segregation tomorrow. Segregation forever," to resounding applause, in 1963. The "whites only" signs have ceased to lurk[1] over water fountains, bathrooms, and restaurant counters.

Yet, 21st-century segregation exists overtly in our school systems, communities, and prisons. It also permeates[2] our society in ways we don't even realize.

We need to continue the conversation about the shocking segregation in our schools and neighborhoods. According to a study last year, 43 % of Latinos and 38 % of blacks go to schools where less than 10 % of their peers are white. But beyond that, we often fail to talk about how segregation impacts us personally. How it <u>permeates</u> not only many of our public and private institutions, but American culture at large. We less easily talk about cultural or social segregation, an area that we have control over, via the restaurants we patronize, the bars we drink at and the places where we worship.

It's time for us to face the reality that for many Americans, even if we live and work around "diversity", our best friends and spiritual leaders, the people we invite into our lives and homes, often look like we do, reinforcing a de facto segregation. This social and cultural segregation isn't restricted to "uneducated" people living in the country. It is equally prominent in environments where smart, educated people are supposed to "know better". People who have studied race, spent months abroad in India or Africa, tasted the best fufu and mofongo, read Ralph Ellison, James Baldwin and Pablo Neruda, and who may even have black "friends" or lovers, still too often manage to have a community that doesn't reflect diversity in their broader city or nation.

[…]

My knee-jerk reaction[3] is to blame racism and discrimination. To complain about all the times that I've felt odd being the only brown face in the crowd. To get mad about how all the television shows that have casts that look like my family are segregated to the so-called "cable ghettos". To get angry at all the bouncers who say they have a racial quota in hotspots. And to wonder why all the books I like are sitting in a "separate" section … until of course, I realize, I'm guilty of many of the same offenses: I segregate, too.

I think about all the nights I plan out that were based on the racial and ethnic make-up of the crowd I am going out with. If I am hanging with black friends, I likely go to an all-black establishment, where I know my friends will like the music, and the mating potential. If I am hanging out with an all-white crowd, I immediately cross all black locations off the list, not wanting anyone to feel uncomfortable. Instead, I relegate myself to being one of a few blacks in the crowd. If it's going to be a night with mixed company, the venue would be more likely to be up for grabs. But an all-black locale still would probably be out of the question.

This isn't secret intel[4]: many blacks, whites, Latinos, and Asians seem to stick to these same guidelines, too, particularly in New York City, America's supposed great melting pot. There are still two Americas: one for brown people and one for whites, and both are heavily segregated.

If our social worlds were more integrated, perhaps we would see it trickle down to the way we govern and the way we dispense justice[5]. Having some sort of connection, a shared experience is the only way I believe that we can get politicians, police officers, and everyday citizens […] to truly understand race.

It may seem silly to connect major state and federal policies to something as simple as a night on the town, but our experiences are shaped not just by legalese[6] and policy, but also by understanding and interacting with each other. Segregation in the 21st century is not just about being legally and physically separated, but about a cultural separation that still feels like it divides more than it binds.

Reniqua Allen, "Our 21st-century segregation: we're still divided by race", on: theguardian.com, 3 April 2013. http://www.theguardian.com/commentisfree/2013/apr/03/21st-century-segregation-divided-race, © Guardian News & Media Ltd 2023

Wortangaben:
1 to lurk: to wait quietly or secretly for sth to happen or sb to appear, usually with bad intentions
2 to permeate: to be present everywhere
3 knee-jerk reaction: way of automatically responding to sth
4 intel: short for intelligence, "insider" information acquired by well-informed sources
5 to dispense justice: to decide whether or not sb is guilty of a criminal act and how this person should be punished
6 legalese: all the special words and expressions that belong to the terminology of judges and lawyers

Lösungsvorschlag

1

> **TIPP**
>
> Here you are supposed to outline a development, which means that you should summarise it concisely without quoting from the text. It might be helpful to structure your text by contrasting the state-enforced segregation of the 1960s with the "voluntary" cultural and individual segregation that the author claims exists today.
> - segregation in the 1960s:
>   - prescribed by law
>   - Black and White people separated spatially
>   *The words "Black" and "White" are capitalised in the following solutions to signal that they are not natural categories but social ones (for more background information on this topic see for example https://www.theatlantic.com/ideas/archive/ 2020/06/time-to-capitalize-blackand-white/613159/).*
> - segregation today:
>   - overt segregation in institutions
>   - self-imposed segregation in personal lives
>   → more implicit, often not admitted
>   - tendency to surround oneself with people from the same ethnicity
>   → impact on social and cultural life
>   - could be overcome through more interaction with people from other backgrounds

The article "Our 21st-Century Segregation: We're Still Divided by Race" by Reniqua Allen, published on the website of *The Guardian*, is about segregation in the US. According to the author, segregation still exists in the 21st century but it is now a culturally motivated separation that people choose freely.	**introduction:** source and topic
Up until the 1960s, segregation was prescribed by law: Black and White Americans were not allowed to eat at the same places or use the same toilets, for example.	**main part:** segregation in the 1960s
While it is no longer state-enforced, the author claims that segregation is still found in public institutions, such as schools or prisons. Even more importantly, however, it exists in people's private lives, impacting society and culture. The reason for this is that people tend to surround themselves with members of their own ethnicity and go to places where they are among "their own". As this new segregation comes from the inside rather than the outside, people are likely to deny it because by admitting to its existence, they would have to admit that they contribute to the phenomenon as well.	segregation today
On the other hand, the author claims that this kind of segregation could be overcome through individual effort, by means of common experiences and more social interaction with people from other racial backgrounds. *(211 words)*	

2 TIPP

This analysis task is twofold: You should both present the author's attitude towards segregation and explain <u>how</u> she conveys it. Structure your answer with regard to content (her general assessment of the modern kind of segregation, her initial angry reaction, her blaming of herself) and support each point with evidence from the text.

- personal attachment to the subject:
  - use of first-person pronoun; reflection on her position as a Black person (cf. e. g. ll. 38/39)
  - repetition of "permeate" (ll. 9, 13) to show the all-pervasiveness of the topic
- wish to raise awareness and call for change
  - address to readers to take action (cf. ll. 10, 17)
  - reference to a study about school segregation (cf. ll. 11/12)
    → credibility
  - dismantling of politically correct behaviour as a mere pretence: interest in other cultures (cf. ll. 17–25), foreign foods (cf. l. 23) and literature by Black or foreign authors (cf. ll. 23/24), but segregation in private life
- anger about modern segregation, but also self-criticism
  - examples of her own experiences with segregation (cf. ll. 27–32)
  - repetition/enumeration of verbs (ll. 27–31) → underlines frustration
  - use of verb "to segregate" in active rather than passive voice (l. 33)
    → stresses individual responsibility
  - examples of how she segregates, too (ll. 34–41)
- conclusion: call for more interaction (cf. ll. 46–54)

The author's attitude towards the modern kind of segregation is conveyed in different ways. *(introduction)*

First of all, Allen writes in the first-person singular, which emphasises how deeply she is affected by the subject of racial segregation. Being Black herself (cf. e. g. ll. 38/39), her private life is as much influenced by segregation as the society she lives in; that this influence is extensive is hinted at by the repeated use of "permeate" (ll. 9, 13). Like everybody else, she claims not to have been particularly aware of the presence of segregation in everyday life (cf. l. 9), which makes it very difficult to fight against. The result is a society that lacks the diversity it officially ensures. *(main part: personal attachment)*

Now that the author has realised that there are "two Americas" (l. 44) existing next to each other without overlapping very often, she wants to make society aware of the lie many Americans are living: her article is like a wake-up call to make her fellow citizens see what they refuse to acknowledge (cf. l. 1). She urgently wants to force them to take action now. Thus, she writes that "[w]e need to continue the conversation about the shocking segregation in our schools" (l. 10) *(wish to raise the readers' awareness)* and "[i]t's time for us to face [...] reality" (l. 17). To prove that this is not just her own possibly prejudiced perception of the world, she refers to a study that revealed that schools are still heavily segregated (cf. ll. 11/12). Before talking about her own experiences, the author reveals the politically correct behaviour of the educated US middle class as a mere pretence: people talk about "diversity" (l. 18) and show interest in other cultures without really mixing with them in their private lives (cf. ll. 17–25). She enumerates foreign-sounding foods (cf. l. 23) and intellectually demanding Black or foreign authors (cf. ll. 23/24). Through her description of how "smart, educated people [who] are supposed to 'know better'" (ll. 21/22) include these in their lives, while still staying in their own small, segregated world, she further exemplifies this pretence.

The author does not exclude herself from sharing the responsibility for segregation, although her metaphorical "knee-jerk reaction" (l. 27) – in other words her first impulse – would be to feel victimised. Her fury at the injustice and the fact that people do not seem to have learned from history is still perceptible when she lists her personal experiences (cf. ll. 27–32). That anger is especially emphasised by her use of language: she starts her sentences with the infinitives "To complain about", "To get mad about", "To get angry at", "And to wonder why" (ll. 27–31) to let off steam about the everyday segregation she is confronted with. *[anger about modern segregation]*

However, she counters that enumeration of verbs which express her anger and frustration by blaming herself, using the half-sentence, "until of course, I realize, I'm guilty of many of the same offenses" (l. 32) and the simple, but impressive statement, "I segregate, too" (l. 33). While the verb "to segregate" is normally not used in the active voice, this personalisation of its use underlines her main point: She herself and most Americans are responsible on a very individual level; they get angry but stay passive and fail to change anything. In the subsequent lines (ll. 34–41), she provides examples of her own "offenses" of segregation. Obviously, she leads a very active social life with friends of different races and carefully selects locations according to the ethnic background of the people she meets. The reasons she gives for her choices are that she does not want non-Black people to feel uncomfortable in an all-Black crowd and that she is rather willing to be the outsider instead (cf. ll. 37–41). *[self-criticism]*

Especially in the light of her own experiences, her final conclusion becomes understandable: change must come from the individual level and "trickle down" (l. 46) to state institutions. In other words, the author believes that political and legal guidelines are only theory as long as they are not based on real-life, multiracially shared ex- *[**conclusion:** call for more interaction]* perience. By including examples from her own life and her own mistakes, she makes her article an appeal to herself and others to be that driving force for change. *(712 words)*

3.1 TIPP

This task requires writing a comment on a statement from the text by including some statistics given and using your own background knowledge. Keep in mind that you need to present your arguments in a structured and coherent way. As a conclusion, you should come to a personal evaluation of the statement.

Possible structure:
- sketching the current situation in the US: progress in interracial relationships, but a lot still has to be done (transition to the statement from the text)
- explanation of the statement: diversity in personal relationships does not yet reflect diversity in society
- backing up the statement with statistics
- giving examples of obstacles that prevent closer interracial contact, mainly between Blacks and Whites
- giving examples of what has to change on a personal and on a societal level
- conclusion: final assessment of Allen's statement

The US has become more diverse in the last few decades, mostly due to immigration from Mexico, South America or Asia. Furthermore, the official, political segregation that existed right into the 1960s is fortunately a thing of the past. It has become more normal for people from different racial or ethnic backgrounds to meet or mix. However, a lot has still to be done to achieve a truly equal society not only on a political but also on a personal level.	**introduction** current situation
The gist of the statement from the text is that people of the same background would rather stick together, although they may be generally open and interested in people from other races and ethnicities, and although they do have some close personal relationships. However, on the whole, the number of interracial personal relationships does not yet reflect the diversity of society in general.	**main part** explanation of the statement
As far as romantic relationships are concerned, for example, US statistics show that there is a certain number of intermarriages, although there are conspicuous differences between the various ethnicities. Marrying outside one's racial or ethnic background is highest among Native Americans, Asian Americans and Hispanics, whereas Black (17 %) and White people (9 %) have the lowest percentage of marrying outside their own group, which seems to support the statement from the text that mingling only seems to go so far. So, what could be the reasons for this?	intermarriages: statistics and interpretation

The advances in political equality do not necessarily promote personal relationships between White and Black people, in particular, as the legacy of slavery and segregation still has a huge impact on educational opportunities and economic status, for example. Still, many neighbourhoods in the US are not really mixed, with White people often wanting to keep to themselves, fearing a loss in value of their properties due to prejudiced attitudes about multi-ethnic neighbourhoods. As far as education is concerned, there is no official segregation anymore, but the above-mentioned still existent racially segregated neighbourhoods often translate into segregated schools too. So, when it comes to education and housing, Black people are still underprivileged, and the socio-economic gap between White and Black Americans stands in the way of more personal contact. *[obstacles that prevent more personal interracial contact]*

As Allen writes in her article, sticking to your own group when going out, for example, is often more convenient and much less hassle than going out with a mixed group. Overcoming this habit can take an effort, but it could be easier if there was more progress on an economic and social level, which would promote contact and therefore understanding as there is proof that prejudices and racism stem from lack of contact or physical proximity. It is therefore not enough for people from different racial and ethnic backgrounds to simply know each other on a personal level – there are also certain conditions that need to be met, such as more equality in socioeconomic status and sharing common goals and values. *[prerequisites for more personal interracial contact]*

Allen is right in stating that the personal lives of Americans from different ethnicities could be more integrated, but this cannot be achieved on an individual level alone. Despite the progress of the last few decades, some change is still needed on a wider social and economic level to make people with different backgrounds mingle more and more often. In the end, it can promote understanding, widen your horizons and help overcome racial prejudice. *[conclusion: more economic and political change needed]* *(557 words)*

3.2 TIPP

In this task, you are free to express your own ideas as to the subject of race relations in the US. However, you should pay attention to the characteristics of a letter to the editor. Possible arguments could be:
- progress achieved, but de facto ongoing segregation and inequality
- segregation is nowadays mainly happening in people's minds
- however, to change that, politics and the media, in particular, have the responsibility to present positive role models
- subconscious prejudices need to be broken down
- tightrope act between affirmative action and discrimination

First of all, thank you very much, Ms Allen, for your enlightening article. I would say that I wholeheartedly agree on most points. As you correctly point out, segregation should be a thing of the past by now. The Civil Rights Movement has achieved so much and legally there is no reason why people of different skin colour should still lead "separate, but equal" lives. Discrimination has been outlawed, we even elected an African American as President of our country and yet it would be too simplistic to interpret all these positive developments as ending inequality.	**introduction** progress through Civil Rights Movement
Statistics speak a different language, and it simply cannot be denied that there still is blatant inequality between Black and White people when it comes to wealth, education, housing, the criminal justice system, etc. And if no discriminatory laws can be blamed for these conditions, as was the case in the 1960s, what or who is to blame?	inequality still persists
Once more, I wholeheartedly agree with you that it is not enough to point an accusing finger at others, while in our own minds we all continue to categorise people according to their skin colour, their religion, their sexual orientation or what have you. So, we have to break down those boundaries in our minds in order to effect the real change in our society that is overdue.	**main part** necessity to overcome barriers in the mind
As to how to break down these boundaries, I slightly disagree with your opinion, however. You wrote that people interacting with people from other ethnic backgrounds in a natural and "colour-blind" way would influence larger political decisions. In an ideal world I would agree, but in an ideal world, people would not even have to write articles like yours to bring the ongoing prejudices to the world's attention. The differences between various social and ethnic groups would not even be noticed and people would not categorise establishments as either "Black" or "White".	idea of colour-blindness too idealistic
Unfortunately, however, we do not live in an ideal world. That is why I think politics and the media, in particular, have a duty to act as positive role models for the society at large. In my opinion, it will not work the other way round. Of course, I admit that strategies like affirmative action, racial quotas or politically correct discourse are often tightrope acts because they might lead to an even more strained atmosphere between different social or ethnic groups. Yet, I think they are necessary to overcome our subconscious fears of what is unknown and foreign.	politics and media must be agents of change
All in all, I believe that only by giving people time, by facilitating multiracial encounters and especially by constantly showing them as something positive can the segregation in our minds be overcome. The first important step in the right direction is by addressing the problem and facing reality instead of pretending that an ideal world with no differences has already arrived. *(473 words)*	**conclusion**

Lesen und Schreiben · Übungsaufgabe 3
Baden-Württemberg · Berufliches Gymnasium · Englisch

Aufgabe 1: Integrierte Aufgabe zum Leseverstehen

Outline the difficulties faced by journalists when trying to present objective news. Use your <u>own</u> words.

Aufgabe 2: Textanalyse

Analyse the means the author uses to show that the ideal of reporting truthfully clashes with reality.

Aufgabe 3: Erörterung/Stellungnahme

3.1 Textbezogen und materialbezogen

"[…] we are living in 'what some call the post-factual or post-truth political era' in which 'what you would like to believe always trumps the facts.'" (ll. 30–32)

Comment on the quotation, considering the message conveyed in the cartoon.

© Chris Madden. Cartoonstock

3.2 Themenbezogen

To leave or not to leave? Is it time to quit social media? Write a blog entry.

| Text | **Why media commentary is so crucial when opinions displace facts**

Is truth relevant any longer? Journalists are encouraged to accept the philosophy behind the adage[1] famously coined by the Guardian's CP Scott[2]: comment is free, but facts are sacred. So editors train trainee reporters to "get the facts" (and student journalists are similarly urged to do the same by their tutors). Junior journalists soon learn that "the facts" need assembling into some kind of order and that the process can be complicated. How facts are presented has an importance too. Stories – and that loaded description is itself revealing – are not simple constructions. They involve placing facts in some kind of order and, crucially, omitting some altogether. Even experienced journalists, reporters and subeditors, affect to think that a collection of facts adds up to some kind of truth. And it is widely accepted in our trade that truth-telling is the point of the job. Providing the public with the necessary "information" on which to base their views enables them to make political, economic and social decisions.

Anyone reading newspapers each day or watching TV news or listening to radio bulletins – and especially if doing all three – will know that truth turns out to be a moving target. "The facts" suddenly dissolve. They become little more than propaganda tools as journalists twist them to suit narratives that we realise make a nonsense of the mission to inform. This process, sometimes reduced to a supposed division between objectivity and subjectivity, has a long history. The newspapers of the 19th and 20th centuries were no more "factual" than those published today. Sacrilegious[3] opinions always dominated the facts. Nor should we overlook the one-sidedness of this matter. No reader, viewer and listener – no member of the public – is a blank page. Everyone who consumes the news does so with their views and attendant assumptions in place, and they are difficult to dislodge[4].

For some reason, clearly influenced by undue optimism, it was supposed that the creation of social media would change everything. Mainstream media's spin[5] would be exposed for what it is. By contrast, unmediated media would allow the people to enjoy unvarnished facts, thus allowing "the truth" to emerge at last. Ha! Bah humbug! Practice has made nonsense of the theory. The output on social media is not only less fact-free than that purveyed[6] by the hated MSM[7], it is overly dominated by opinions. The Guardian's leading article today pointed out that we are living in "what some call the post-factual or post-truth political era" in which "what you would like to believe always trumps the facts."

I agree but only up to a point because I take issue with the belief that it is a new phenomenon, a new age. Surely it has always been the case. When Scott wrote his facts-are-sacred essay in 1921, he was already rowing against the tide. Less than a decade before, the opinions of the British people had been moulded[8] – against their prior wishes – to accept the necessity of going to war. And, as Scott knew well enough at one point in the war, sacred facts confided by a journalist to the prime minister, David Lloyd George, about the horrors of the frontline were kept from the public in order to prevent a peace movement gaining hold. That is not to say that Scott's intentions were not honourable. Nor is it to say that we should simply accept the situation and dispense with fact-hunting altogether. But it is hugely important to highlight the fact, yes the fact, that opinions continue to hold sway[9] in all news output. That, of course, is the major role of media commentators: to make transparent to as wide an audience as possible, as often as possible, the underlying messages of so-called facts. I write this in the knowledge that it is a self-serving, self-justifying statement. However, I do so because it concerns me that too few mainstream media outlets now cover the media. This is especially worrying at a time when opinions overshadow facts and at a time of media transition. Facts, as that Guardian editorial said, "need to be tested". Not only that. Given that contested facts – factoids, perhaps? – influence those opinions, it is crucial to provide a running analysis of what lies behind the news.

I accept that plenty of non-journalists use social media to do that, and good for them. Their problem is in gaining the trust of a large enough audience in order to hold the fact-twisters to account[10]. For the foreseeable future, that should be a major task for mainstream media. If journalism is to have any value to society, then it has to analyse itself. What is at issue here is truth and trust. Newspapers may be in their death throes[11], at least in print form. But we must not abandon our task because we know, do we not, the answer to that question about who should guard the guards? *(814 words)*

© *Roy Greenslade, Why media commentary is so crucial when opinions displace facts,*
https://www.theguardian.com/media/greenslade/2016/aug/25/why-media commentary-is-so-crucial-when-op, 25.08.2016

Wortangaben:
1 adage: short statement or proverb
2 CP Scott: Charles Prestwich Scott (1846–1932), British journalist, editor and owner of *The Manchester Guardian* (now *The Guardian*)
3 sacrilegious: treating a holy thing or place without respect
4 to dislodge: to force or knock sth out of its position
5 spin: here: a certain way of presenting information
6 to purvey: to provide, to supply
7 MSM: abbreviation for "mainstream media"
8 to mould: here: to strongly influence someone's opinion
9 to hold sway: to have or exert great control or influence (over sb)
10 to hold to account: to require a person to explain or to accept responsibility for his or her actions
11 throe: violent pain

Lösungen

1 TIPP

This task requires you to name the difficulties journalists face when trying to present news in an objective way. Read the text carefully, highlighting only the relevant aspects. It is essential when summarising that you do not quote from the text but convey the main points in your own words. Do not forget to start your text by mentioning the title, author and topic.

introduction:
- title and author
- topic: presenting news in an objective way is difficult

main part:
- facts are sacred: journalists must tell the truth
- collecting, assembling and sorting facts, however, is subjective
- opinions influence the presentation of facts

conclusion: search for the truth behind the facts is essential

---

In his article "Why media commentary is so crucial when opinions displace facts" in *The Guardian* Roy Greenslade points out that the role of journalists to present objective news has become more important than ever but that it is a difficult undertaking.

introduction
difficult to present news objectively

The author begins his article by asking if truth still plays a role in journalism. The quote 'comment is free, but facts are sacred' illustrates the conviction among journalists that their main job is to tell the truth, which is achieved by keeping to the facts and presenting them to the public. This, however, often proves to be difficult for the following reasons:

main part
journalists' goal: tell the truth

Greenslade questions the widely held view among journalists that assembling facts automatically represents the truth. As the facts need to be put in a certain order and journalists also have to decide what facts to choose to form a narrative there is no absolute truth – it is relative, depending on the writer and also on the reader's preconceptions. Therefore, journalists need to be aware of opinions always having an effect on the presentation of news, and they should make the opinions that lie beneath the facts transparent to the readers.

collecting and assessing facts: subjective

opinions affecting news

Taking all this into account, presenting objective and truthful news is difficult, but, as the author of the article concludes, the search for the truth behind the news must not be given up and journalism has to constantly question itself.

conclusion
self-criticism

(235 words)

2 TIPP

Writing a text analysis requires a close examination of style and register, choice of words and the linguistic devices an author uses to stress certain points and get their message across. After going through the text again carefully, try to find those elements and explain their respective functions in their context.

introduction: in journalism, truth often clashes with reality

main part: stylistic devices to prove the author's point
- starting with provocative question to show that truth is relative, ending with rhetorical question
- quotation marks to express doubt ("the facts", "the truth"), contradicting high ideals of journalism
- choice of vocabulary and register: formal vocabulary as proof of being an expert; sophisticated register interrupted by informal interjections ("humbug", "ha! ba!") to express disapproval; deliberate use of the terms "[s]tories" and "narratives": more fiction than facts
- linguistic devices to emphasise his assertion: alliteration (l. 56), repetition (ll. 42–46), metaphors and personification (ll. 14/15, 36, 48, 56)
- frequent use of pronouns "we" and "our" (author part of the trade), written in the first person (also emphasising his view)
- quoting colleagues and appealing to them (ll. 2/3, ll. 30/31, 49/50)
- historical example to prove that truth can be falsified

conclusion: journalists' task: to analyse and comment

Roy Greenslade, the author of the article, is a journalist himself and knows how to employ various stylistic means effectively to stress his point of view that truth-telling in journalism is a difficult undertaking and that the high ideal of trying to tell the truth often clashes with reality.

introduction
referring to the author's intention

Greenslade gets straight to the point with the provocative question "Is truth relevant any longer?" (l. 1) and he closes his article with a rhetorical question, meaning that it is the journalists themselves who should be critical with their own trade and guard the truth (ll. 57/58). To emphasise that they are relative, he also puts the words "[the] facts" (ll. 3, 5, 15) and "truth" (l. 27) in quotation marks several times. The use of the adjective "so-called" (l. 45) also serves to underline the writer's opinion that there is no absolute truth. In this way, he contradicts the high ideals of journalism expressed in the "philosophy" (l. 1) of "[getting] the facts" (l. 3) and the "mission to inform" (l. 17). As the connection between facts and truth is the topic of the article, both terms occur frequently.

main part
truth is relative: use of questions

expressing doubt: use of quotation marks

contradicting high ideals of journalism

The author also uses rather formal vocabulary in his text like "adage" (l. 2) or "sacrilegious" (l. 19), which show that he is an educated person, addressing an educated audience, and that he, as a journalist, knows how to handle language. He shows this, for example, by suddenly switching from formal to informal register with the (old fashioned) interjection "Ha! Bah humbug!" (l. 27) to express his utter disapproval of the idea that social media would help "'the truth' to emerge" (l. 27), strongly dismissing it as "nonsense" (l. 28). Greenslade also mentions journalists using terms like "stories" (l. 6), or "narratives" (l. 16), which refer to fiction rather than facts. choice of formal and informal vocabulary and register

Greenslade also uses further linguistic devices to emphasise his assertion such as alliteration, for example "truth and trust" (l. 56), repetition, e. g. "the fact, yes the fact" (ll. 42/43), "as wide an audience as possible, as often as possible" (ll. 44/45), or "self-serving, self-justifying" (l. 46). Moreover, he knows how to make his text more vivid by using metaphors and personifications such as "truth turns out to be a moving target" (ll. 14/15), "'The facts' suddenly dissolve" (l. 15), "opinions […] had been moulded" (l. 36), "when opinions overshadow facts" (l. 48), or "newspapers in their death throes" (l. 56). linguistic devices: emphasising his assertion, making text more vivid

Greenslade's frequent use of the personal pronouns "I", "me" and "we" and the possessive determiner "our" has several purposes. He expresses his opinion and his involvement as a reader ("I agree", l. 33, "I take issue", l. 33, "I write", l. 46, "I do so", l. 47, "It concerns me", l. 47) and identifies himself as a journalist ("in our trade", l. 10, "our task", l. 47) at the same time. use of the first person singular and plural

To show he is part of the trade, Greenslade also quotes journalists (ll. 30/31, 49/50) or former journalists (C.P. Scott, ll. 2/3) of *The Guardian*. He also addresses his colleagues by ending his essay with a rhetorical question, admonishing them not only to control and comment on the activities of the people in power, but also to question and scrutinise themselves ("guard the guards", l. 58). quoting colleagues and appealing to them

To prove his point that facts can be withheld by the press, and the truth falsified, Greenslade furthermore mentions the historical example that during the First World War, journalists helped the British government to keep an unpleasant truth secret. mentioning of an historical example

As a journalist, Greenslade knows how to argue convincingly that "facts" and reality often differ from each other, and that it is the journalists' task to analyse and comment on the news and to always be critical with their own work. **conclusion** comment needed

(623 words)

3.1 TIPP

When you are asked to write a comment, you are expected to express your opinion on a certain topic – in this task on a given quotation – after carefully examining the argument or statement presented. First, you have to think about the quote carefully and explain it by considering the context in which it was given. In the next step, you need to describe the cartoon and interpret its message. Then combine the messages of the quotation and the cartoon and say whether you agree or disagree.

introduction: social media did not promote spreading of truth

main part: quotation and cartoon
- explanation of quotation: digital media did not promote the distribution of truth and facts, they created "the post-factual or post-truth political era" (l. 31)
- message of the cartoon: social media platforms misguide users
- connection between quote and cartoon: quotation and cartoon convey the same message: social media spread propaganda, conspiracy theories and fake news; distorting facts, however, not a recent phenomenon

conclusion:
- the quotation and the cartoon draw attention to a dangerous and detrimental development
- responsible journalists as guardians of the truth more necessary than ever

---

When it was first developed there was a lot of optimism that social media, or "unmediated media", would make it easier for facts and sincere truths to spread. However, it turned out that it rather contributed to the distribution of opinions and fake news. **introduction**

Greenslade uses a quotation from a *Guardian* article which describes the situation. Instead of promoting "unvarnished facts" (l. 27), social media created "the post-factual or post-truth political era" (l. 30/31). More often than not, content on the internet is not objective but biased, and facts are distorted and untruths circulate. The quotation describes a political culture in which debates are dominated by claims and appeals to emotion, and which affect not only individuals but also society as a whole. **main part**
explanation of the quotation

The cartoon illustrates this development and shows how social media can lead people astray. It depicts two men who are ignoring a sign on which "truth" is written. They are, however, following instructions on social media and are heading in the opposite direction of the truth. One of the men is looking back and seems to have his doubts about believing the social media instructions, which say that "truth is a conspiracy", while the man in front is off and away, convinced that social media is showing him the right way. explanation of the cartoon

The cartoonist's message is quite clear: social media misguides people. They readily believe unmediated content on the internet and are prone to propaganda, conspiracy theories, disinformation, and blatant lies. This is precisely what the quotation "what you would like to believe always trumps the facts" (l. 31 f.) expresses. As a result, a lot of social media users retweet what they believe to be true, but in reality spread rumours, judgements and opinions. In this way, they influence and reinforce the opinions or prejudices of other users. Greenslade, however, notes that this is not a recent and unprecedented phenomenon by referring to a historic effort to mould public opinion in pre-digital times (cf. l. 36).

In my view, the quotation and the cartoon point to a dangerous and detrimental development of free discourse in our society. I believe that the increase in propaganda, distorted news, harassment, and hate mails on the platforms polarise and divide society. In this critical situation, the task of journalists, as Greenslade defines it, has become more relevant and indispensable: to uncover and analyse "what lies behind the news" (l. 51). In this way, responsible journalists act as guardians of the truth and help people distinguish between misinformation and plausibility.

(418 words)

message of the cartoon and relation to the quotation

conclusion
need for critical journalism

3.2 TIPP

When writing a blog, think about who you want to reach. To attract your readers' attention, create a catchy headline or questions to arouse interest in your entry. Also structure your text in paragraphs and make your text attractive by detailing your personal experiences with social media. Include stylistic devices to address your readers directly (e. g. salutation, questions, conversational phrases or question tags).

introduction: celebrities leaving social media, transition to own experience

main part:
- negative sides: reasons for leaving social media:
  - wish to take a break
  - developing impolite habits, bad behaviour
  - offensive language, abusive posts, fake news
  - wasting too much time
  - danger of misuse of personal data
- positive sides: reasons for staying
  - desire to receive positive reactions
  - curiosity about friends' lives
  - new and interesting connections
- conclusion: undecided: keep account open?

Hi everyone,

Are you concerned about your social media usage? Are you even thinking of leaving Instagram or Twitter? Some celebrities have done that recently, and I'm having second thoughts as well. Let me tell you why.

I'm certainly not one of those famous people, but just like them, I want to take a break because I realised I've become dependent on social networking because I'm constantly checking my accounts. I feel like a drug addict. There's not a minute I don't check my account. Every ping gets me excited, and I can't resist checking what the message may be about. What about you? Do you do the same?

I've also adopted a somewhat impolite habit. Like many of my friends, I always keep my mobile phone within reach. It's not nice, I know, when you are in company. My partner, who is not really into social media, is very annoyed by that. It's rude and disrespectful, but it's very common these days. Sometimes you see four or five people sitting at a table and everyone is staring at their phone. Psychologists say we are programmed to respond to these devices without realising we're being rude. It's just the habitual use that triggers us to respond immediately. Even so, this might be an explanation, but it's certainly not an excuse for behaving poorly.

That loss of good behaviour is also reflected in the way people express themselves on the net. Many people believe they are invisible and unreachable, which is why they use offensive language, swear words and expletives. Etiquette has been eroded, don't you agree? In addition, I've been receiving more and more abusive and unpleasant comments lately. It's very frustrating, to say the least. I'm really fed up with all the hate mails and also the flood of fake news. It's hard to believe what stupid stuff, such as ridiculous theories and outrageous conspiracies, people post on the net. I think this could be another turning point for me.

My friends also keep reminding me I'm wasting too much time watching nonsense, like all those videos on TikTok. Yes, I suppose it is true. It's hard for me, though, to stop scrolling through the app. I'm just addicted, you could say.

Another point to consider is that feeding digital companies with loads of personal data is a real danger because we just don't know what the giant data gatherers will do with our personal details. I've often read reports of misuse of personal information or that accounts have been hacked.

So, why haven't you stopped using social media, you might ask. What still keeps me social networking is that I rather like receiving positive feedback on my posts. I've got to admit that. What is more important, however, is that I want to see what my friends are doing.

	introduction celebrities quitting social media
	main part transition to own experience
	reasons to leave social media: bad habits when in company
	offensive language and abusive posts fake news
	waste of time
	potential misuse of personal data
	reasons to stay: positive feedback and curiosity as reasons to stay

Through my communication on the platforms, I've also met a lot of interesting people from all over the world. With some of them, even real friendships have been formed because we share the same hobbies and interests. It would be very difficult to give up these connections. — *new connections*

Considering all of that, there seem to be more negative than positive sides to using social media, and I can understand that some people have good reasons for closing their accounts. However, I'm still reluctant to leave now, as I enjoy being in touch with the world and being in close contact with my friends. I'm not sure what I'll do in the end, but I've taken a first step: I've resolved not to post so often and keep a low profile for a while. What do you think? What are you going to do? Do let me know! — **conclusion**

(618 words)

Lesen und Schreiben · Übungsaufgabe 4
Baden-Württemberg · Berufliches Gymnasium · Englisch

Aufgabe 1: Integrierte Aufgabe zum Leseverstehen

Summarise the demands and suggestions directed by the UNHCR and the IOM to the European Union. Use your <u>own</u> words.

Aufgabe 2: Textanalyse

Analyse the stylistic means used in the text to show that a reform of the EU's migration management is necessary.

Aufgabe 3: Erörterung / Stellungnahme

3.1 Textbezogen und materialbezogen

"Saving lives must be a priority and not impeded or criminalized." (ll. 24/25)

Comment on this statement also considering the information given in the graph and the text.

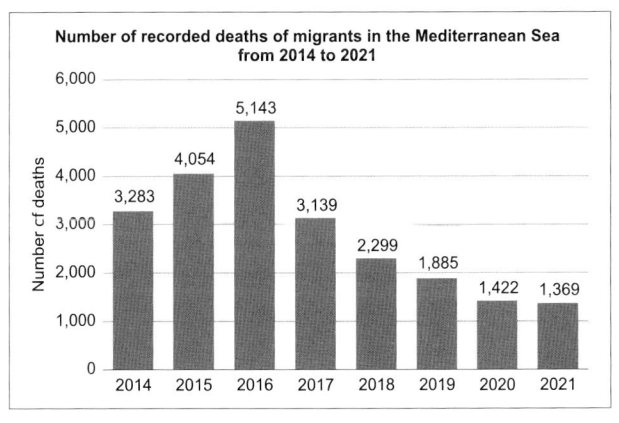

Number of recorded deaths of migrants in the Mediterranean Sea from 2014 to 2021

Year	Number of deaths
2014	3,283
2015	4,054
2016	5,143
2017	3,139
2018	2,299
2019	1,885
2020	1,422
2021	1,369

© *Statista*

3.2 Themenbezogen

"For migrants, language is the key to integration." vs. "The importance of language for integration is exaggerated."

In a podcast, Harriet Aiken, the host of the podcast, and Shailesh Patel, a lecturer in sociolinguistics, talk about the importance of language for integration. Write the dialogue.

| Text | **UNHCR and IOM call for a truly common and principled approach to European migration and asylum policies**

On the eve of the launch of the presentation of the European Commission's new Pact on Migration and Asylum, UNHCR, the UN Refugee Agency, and IOM, the International Organization for Migration, are appealing to the European Union (EU) to ensure a truly joint and principled approach that addresses all aspects of migration and asylum governance. The two UN bodies are hopeful that the Pact will provide a fresh start to move from an ad hoc crisis-driven approach to asylum and migration in Europe to a common one that is more comprehensive, well-managed and predictable, both within and beyond the EU. [...]

[...] Events across the Mediterranean, including delays in disembarking migrants and refugees rescued at sea, increasing reports of pushbacks and the devastating fires at the Moria Registration and Identification Centre (RIC) on the Greek island of Lesvos [in 2020], have further highlighted the urgent need to reform the EU's management of migration and asylum. COVID-19 has also heavily affected relevant policies and practices, and its detrimental socio-economic impact has not spared anyone. Refugees, migrants and large refugee hosting countries around the world, have been particularly affected.

The current approach in the EU is unworkable, untenable and often carries devastating human consequences. With the lack of EU-wide agreement on disembarkation exacerbating human suffering, the organizations have been jointly calling for a common EU action to take responsibility for search and rescue, and for disembarking people rescued at sea. IOM and UNHCR strongly agree with European Commission President Ursula von der Leyen that saving lives at sea is not optional [...]. The organizations also extend concern for those along all migration routes who find themselves endangered, including on land. Saving lives must be the priority and should not be impeded or criminalized.

UNHCR and IOM have also called for more predictable arrangements on relocation within the EU, and actively supported [...] relocations from the Greek islands, working with the Greek Government, the European Commission, EASO[1] and UNICEF, the UN Children's Fund. The relocation of vulnerable people, including children, especially at a time of heightened hardship, has proven to be a workable example of responsibility sharing.

[...] Most migration to Europe is managed through safe and legal channels, and the COVID-19 crisis has highlighted the value of migrant and refugee workers in the EU and elsewhere. Their contributions and potential should be maximized. Well-managed human mobility will not only be instrumental in recovering from the pandemic, however. It should also be mainstreamed and inform longer-term policy and responses, including climate change, as well as support flexible and dynamic labour markets.

[...] Progress on fighting smuggling and enhancing humanitarian border management can be achieved with equal attention and resources devoted to strengthening and broadening legal migration and safe pathways, genuine partnerships, integration and building prosperous, healthy, cohesive communities. It can also reduce the demand that feeds the business of criminal smuggling groups. Investing in regular migration channels and enhanced mobility will also be essential to sustainable development and growth in the EU and elsewhere.

Dignified returns, for those who wish to return to their countries of origin or who are found not to be in need of international or other forms of protection, are equally crucial to a well-managed, comprehensive system. Voluntary returns should be prioritized and include provisions for sustainable reintegration. Some migrants, including victims of trafficking, sexual abuse and unaccompanied children, who are found not in need of asylum may have a legitimate need for other forms of assistance and protection.

The EU's commitment to predictable global solidarity and responsibility sharing in partnership with large refugee-hosting countries outside the EU is also welcomed. This commitment has to be translated into action with additional, predictable and flexible financial assistance and political support to hosting states, including to strengthen their asylum systems. This will ensure migrants and refugees have adequate access to services, such as health, education and work, so they can live their lives in dignity. More strategic support to countries hosting the largest numbers of refugees or transit countries would also diminish the appeal of being smuggled.

With a viable future and greater commitment from EU countries to resettlement, complementary pathways and family reunification, coupled with the conditions to ensure direct access to territory and asylum in the EU for those who need it, fewer people might resort to dangerous journeys and states will be better able to manage arrivals. […] *(729 words)*

© *https://www.unhcr.org/news/press/2020/9/5f69deff4/unhcr-iom-call-truly-common-principled-approach-european-migration-asylum.htm*

Wortangabe:
1 EASO: European Asylum Support Office agency

Lösungen

1 TIPP

In this task, you need to write a brief summary of a press release from two UN organisations, UNHCR and IOM, which focus on assisting refugees and campaigning for the rights of asylum seekers. Before you start working on the assignment, read the text carefully. It is essential to have a good understanding of the arguments of the two agencies to write a solution in which you should use your own words. Do not quote or copy from the text, and do not include your opinion. In the introduction's topic mention the sources of the statement and their main aim. Use the simple present tense.

introduction:
- press release of migration agencies UNHCR and IOM
- aim: demand for migration reform

main part:
- coordinated and comprehensive approach necessary
- support of relocation programmes and migrant workers needed
- key to more humane migration system: strengthening legal migration
- important: further cooperation with refugees hosting countries outside the EU

conclusion: improved migration policy will save lives

In a press release, two agencies of the United Nations demand a reform of the European Union's management of migration and integration of refugees. Several tragic events in the Mediterranean, including drownings at sea and a fire in a refugee camp, highlighted the urgency for action to be taken.

The UNHCR and the International Organization for Migration (IOM) criticise the EU's current approach to dealing with the issue of immigration. Rather than reacting only in emergencies, and in an uncoordinated way, the EU should introduce a common, comprehensive, and dependable migration system.

A common approach would be to share responsibility by relocating vulnerable people, e. g. from the Greek islands. Relocation programmes should be intensified as should the support of people who help migrants and refugees.

For the UNHCR and the IOM legal migration is the key to a more humane migration system, so it should be strengthened and expanded to keep refugees safe and stop the trafficking of people. The migration organisations emphasise that not only European countries will benefit from legal and safe migration.

introduction
demand for migration reform

main part
coordinated and comprehensive approach

support of relocation programmes and migrant workers

strengthening legal migration

The UN agencies moreover say it is important to help people who want to go back to their home countries, and migrants who have had bad experiences. The UNHCR and the IOM appreciate the EU's co-operation with countries that host large numbers of refugees outside the EU and demand greater political and financial support for them. In the end, these demands and suggestions are aiming at improving migration management, which will save lives and facilitate the transfer of refugees. *(252 words)*

strengthening cooperation with refugee hosting countries

conclusion

2 TIPP

To write a text analysis, it is important to identify the source and the recipient. The text in question was written by two migration agencies, which are concerned about the safety of refugees and asylum seekers. Their statement is an appeal for an improved EU migration policy. To this end, they present a number of suggestions and demands. They use various stylistic devices to emphasise the urgency of adopting a new pact in order to avoid further deaths on migration routes. Go through the text and mark such means, e. g. choice of words or repetitions, which are intended to emphasise it is high time to act.

introduction: appeal to EU to reform migration procedures: urgency to act

main part:
- choice of words (adjectives, verbs, nouns):
  - words with negative connotations to describe plight of refugees and EU failure and to show urgency for reform, e. g. "crisis-driven approach" (l. 6), "devastating fires" (l. 10), "exacerbating human suffering" (l. 19), "delays" (l. 9), "pushbacks" (l. 10)
  - words (adjectives) with positive connotations (often enumerated) to emphasise message, e. g. "comprehensive, well-managed and predictable […]" (l. 7), "building prosperous, healthy, cohesive communities" (l. 41)
- repetition of key words and use of modals to stress importance to act, e. g. "well-managed", "joint/jointly", "common" and "comprehensive", "should" (ll. 24, 34, 36, 47), "must", "has to" and "have to" (ll. 24, 53 and 55)
- citation of president of EU commission to reveal gap between ideal and reality

conclusion: strong and impressive plea

The text is an appeal of the UNHCR and IOM, two migration agencies of the United Nations, directed towards the European Union, putting pressure on the EU to reform its haphazard and defective migration procedures. To illustrate the urgency of a change in policy and to emphasise what must be done to achieve it various stylistic devices are employed in the text.

introduction
appeal to EU
urgency to act

First of all, the plight of the refugees and the failure of EU policy is described in dramatic words. Here, numerous words and phrases with a negative connotation are used, e. g. adjectives like in "crisis-driven approach" (l. 6), "devastating fires" (l. 10), "detrimental socio-economic impact" (l. 14), "[approach] is unworkable, untenable and often carries devastating human consequences" (ll. 17/18), "exacerbating human suffering" (l. 19), "endangered" (l. 24) and "impeded or criminalized" (l. 25). Nouns like "delays" (l. 9), "push-backs" (l. 10), "lack [of EU-wide agreement]" (l. 18) and "hardship" (l. 30) serve a similar purpose, so there should be no question that there is "urgent need to reform" (l. 12). **main part**
choice of words: negative connotations to show urgency for reform

What must be done by the EU to change this unbearable situation is described with positively connotated adjectives, which are often enumerated to give the UN organisations' message more emphasis, for example "comprehensive, well-managed and predictable [...]" (l. 7), "building prosperous, healthy, cohesive communities" (l. 41), "additional, predictable and flexible financial assistance" (ll. 53/54) and "viable future" (l. 59). They describe the alternative procedures to which the EU must commit – the noun "commitment" being repeated three times in the final paragraphs. Other key words which are repeated in the text and stand for what EU migration policy should be like, are "well-managed", "joint/jointly", "common" and "comprehensive". With the repeated usage of the modals "should" (ll. 24, 34, 36, 47), "must", "has to" and "have to" (ll. 24, 53 and 55) the urgency for the EU to act is stressed further and crucial improvements are called for. positive connotations, enhanced by enumeration to emphasise message

emphasis by repetition of key words and use of modals

The appeal serves to remind the EU of its humane ideals by also taking Ursula von der Leyen, the European Commission President, at her word, who stated that saving lives at sea is not optional (cf. ll. 21/22), to which the EU, however, has still to live up to. citation of president of EU commission

All in all, the UN organisations' appeal is a very strong and impressive plea which was written to be heard. *(393 words)* **conclusion**

3.1 TIPP

The assignment requires a comment in which you combine the message of the quote with the data of the chart given. First, find out the context of the quote: It is part of the statement with which the EU commission presented its improved migration and asylum policy. Second, interpret the graph which shows the number of migrant deaths in the Mediterranean until 2021. Finally, describe the relation between the statement and the graph. The bar chart presents the bare facts, and behind those facts lie the human tragedies which, according to the statement of the EU, must be avoided at all costs. However, there is a deep rift between the EU's humanitarian ideals and the reality on the Mediterranean Sea as the UN organisations point out in the text.

introduction: EU migration policy fails to save lives, untenable situation to criminalise rescue missions

main part:
- inhumane circumstances in refugee camps
- voyage across the sea: most dangerous migration route
- relation to the graph: reveals high number of drownings
- work of NGO rescue ships obstructed or rescuers imprisoned
- demand (see quote): sea rescue must not be punished

conclusion:
- protection for migrants urgently needed
- EU must establish a common and humane migration policy

Particularly since the peak of the migration crisis of 2015/16 shocking news of migrants in distress at sea and bodies washed ashore in the Mediterranean Sea have made plain a humanitarian disaster the EU has not been able to cope. This untenable situation proves the point of the UNHCR and the IOM that the European Union's current approach to migration does not save lives and rather impedes and criminalises rescue at sea (cf. l. 25).

introduction
EU migration policy does not save lives

Refugees and migrants flee from poverty, persecution or war to seek safety and a better life in Europe, with their dangerous journey often ending in refugee camps, where they hope to be able to apply for asylum. The untenable situation in those camps, culminating in "devastating fires" (l. 10) in one of these camps further "highlighted the urgent need to reform" (l. 12) of the EU migration system.

main part
dangerous journey and untenable situation in refugee camps

Although the UN organisations "extend concern for those along all migration routes who find themselves endangered, including on land" (ll. 23/24), the most dangerous migration route, however, is across the sea. A bar chart shows the number of recorded deaths of migrants in the Mediterranean Sea from 2014 to 2021. In 2014, more

voyage across the sea: most dangerous migration route
relation to the graph

than 3,000 people drowned, rising to 4,054 people in 2015 and reaching a peak in 2016, during the height of the "migration crisis", when over 5,000 people lost their lives at sea. At that time, large numbers of Syrian refugees fleeing the war in their home country, and refugees from African countries set out on the dangerous voyage to Italy or Greece. Many were driven into the hands of people traffickers who supplied rusty boats or rubber-dinghies which were completely unsuited to cope with the perils at sea. In the years that followed, the numbers of those who drowned decreased to figures below those of 2014, yet the current number is still unbearable, and is actually on the rise again.

To lower the still large numbers of drownings, it was often ships funded by NGOs that rescued shipwrecked migrants. The work of the rescuers, however, has constantly been "impeded or criminalized" (cf. l. 25) as it is seen by authorities, e. g. in Italy, as a "pull factor" which makes migrants embark on the dangerous journey in the first place. The governments and authorities of the EU countries most affected by migration therefore often respond with harsh methods to discourage refugees and reduce or stop the influx. However, the tightening of border controls, "delays in disembarking migrants" (l. 9) and increase of pushbacks (cf. l. 10) made things worse. Quite often the NGO vessels were not allowed to enter a port in Italy, and it also happened that captains and crew of the boats were put on trial. That is why European Commission President Ursula von der Leyen said that saving lives at sea is not optional (cf. ll. 21/22), and that the UN migration bodies demanded that sea rescue should not be punished. NGO rescue ships, reaction of Mediterranean EU members

The plea of the UNHCR and IOM shows that the EU still lacks a common, comprehensive und humane migration policy. People who are forced to flee their homes and seek safety must be protected and treated with dignity. Saving lives is an obligation, not an option, as von der Leyen pointed out. conclusion EU to establish a common and humane migration policy

(545 words)

3.2 TIPP

This is a task that requires creativity. You are free to develop arguments for or against the importance of language for integration. There are two characters introduced in the assignment, Harriet Aiken and Shailesh Patel, and their respective functions. Attribute to these people the divergent views about the topic. It seems probable that Patel, the linguist, is more knowledgeable about the subject, while the podcaster might rather voice the arguments brought forward by people "in the street". Since this is a podcast, you should present the diverse opinions as a lively exchange of views between host and guest, always keeping to etiquette, which is polite in tone.

introduction: podcaster introduces guest and topic of discussion

starting point: divergent views, pros: language is the key to integration, cons: importance of language for integration exaggerated

main part:

pros:
- language essential for taking part in the everyday life of the host country, proof: today schools use various methods to teach newcomers language of the host country
- language necessary for success in life (job, friendships, etc.)
- language gives an insight into another culture

cons:
- immigrants often integrated successfully without knowing the language of their new homeland, proof: immigrants in the past (19th century)
- integration works best if newcomers are allowed to keep their own language, proof in history: bilingual education

conclusion: common agreement: language is not the main and only key to integration, an open mind is also needed

---

Harriet Aiken: Hello everyone. Today's topic is the importance of language for integration. With me today is Mr Shailesh Patel, a lecturer in sociolinguistics. Is language necessary for integration, Mr. Patel? *(introduction of topic)*

Shailesh Patel: Well, I think that language is the key to integration. *(exchanging pros and cons)*

Harriet Aiken: But isn't the importance of language for integration exaggerated?

Shailesh Patel: Why should it be?

Harriet Aiken: There are enough examples of people who integrated successfully, although they could not speak the language of their new country.

Shailesh Patel: OK, could you give me an example?

Harriet Aiken: Just look at the masses of immigrants who went to America in the 19th century from all parts of the world – from Italy, Germany or Eastern Europe – they didn't know any English. They spoke German, Polish or Italian, and there were no language classes for them to go to. They got along quite well in their new homeland without English proficiency.

Shailesh Patel: That may have been true in the beginning, but if you want to take part in the everyday life of your host country and be fully integrated you need to be able to communicate fluently, or at least have some knowledge of the language.

Harriet Aiken: OK, that's right, but still my point is that integration is also possible without learning the new language. It works best if newcomers are allowed to keep their own language, and there is proof in history.

Shailesh Patel: Not quite. I know what you mean. You are referring to California in the 1970s and 80s when immigrant children were taught in their mother tongue, which in most cases was Spanish, to facilitate integration.

Harriet Aiken: Yes, that's right.

Shailesh Patel: May I remind you that the children were also taught in English? "Bilingual education" was the name. The system has changed over the years. Today, schools can choose the way they see as appropriate for their students to learn English more swiftly, but – and this proves my point – the main aim was and still is to enable newcomers to master the new language. The method, be it bilingual or immersion, is rather irrelevant.

Harriet Aiken: I see your point. I'm just saying that language is not the main and only key to integration. Other qualities or abilities are equally relevant.

Shailesh Patel: Like what?

Harriet Aiken: Tolerance and an open mind, for example. As a newcomer, you must be prepared to accept new and different ways of doing things. You must be willing to learn, perhaps change or get rid of old habits – without losing or giving up your heritage.

Shailesh Patel: I couldn't agree more. What you are saying is all very well, but I still insist that language is the main and most important factor if integration is to succeed. Immigrants must be able to express themselves in the language of the country. Only then can they get a proper job, make friends, or start a business.

Harriet Aiken: Yes, I can see that, but …

Shailesh Patel: May I add another point? Apart from the fact that language is so important for a person to communicate and succeed economically, language also gives an insight into another culture because it transports ideas and values, so it helps people cope with the challenge of culture clash most immigrants are confronted with.

Harriet Aiken: OK, perhaps we could meet half-way, meaning I accept that language is important, but it's not the only key to integration. *compromise*

Shailesh Patel: Of course not, I believe that the other qualities you mentioned are just as relevant. *(555 words)*

PRÜFUNGSAUFGABEN

Offizielle Musterprüfung

Baden-Württemberg • Berufliches Gymnasium • Englisch

TEIL I: HÖRVERSTEHEN   25 VP

You will hear each recording twice. After each listening, you will have time to complete your answers.

Task 1: 3D printing   5 BE

You will hear five speakers talking about technique and the applications of 3D printing. While listening, match the headings A to G with the speakers 1 to 5. There are two more headings than you need.
You now have time to read the assignment.

	Heading
A	trivial application
B	various processes
C	technical problems
D	environmental impact
E	dangerous perspective
F	empowered individuals
G	prestigious personalisation

Speaker	1	2	3	4	5
Heading					

Now listen to the recording again.

| Task 2: Auto industry | 8 BE |

Listen to the following podcast about car manufacturers in the USA.
While listening, tick (✓) the correct answer (a, b or c). There is only one correct answer.
You now have time to read the assignment.

1 There is a lack of computer chips in the car industry because its suppliers …
  a ☐ had to fight the pandemic.
  b ☐ couldn't meet the rising need.
  c ☐ needed semiconductors themselves.

2 As a consequence General Motors had to …
  a ☐ close two factories forever.
  b ☐ lay off workers temporarily.
  c ☐ stop production for some time.

3 At the moment, some major car manufacturers, like Honda and Toyota, are …
  a ☐ not affected worldwide.
  b ☐ not affected in North America.
  c ☐ heavily affected in North America.

4 In the near future, car manufacturers will …
  a ☐ face a situation even worse.
  b ☐ face bigger issues than semiconductors.
  c ☐ see more semiconductors on the market.

5 If companies have enough semiconductors, they can …
  a ☐ be optimistic.
  b ☐ still be affected seriously.
  c ☐ re-open some of their factories.

6 For the car manufacturers the delay in the production of cars means facing …
  a ☐ a tight schedule.
  b ☐ a loss of a million cars.
  c ☐ a reduction in revenues.

7 For potential car buyers it means …
  a ☐ no delivery.
  b ☐ better options.
  c ☐ limited choices.

8 For the Biden administration, fighting this crisis …
  a ☐ will take some time.
  b ☐ is the task of national car makers.
  c ☐ can only be solved internationally.

Now listen to the recording again.

| Task 3: Attacks on minorities (FBI report) | 12 BE |

You will hear an interview about an FBI report (Federal Bureau of Investigation) that deals with hate crime. While listening, take notes on the following points. You need not write complete sentences. You now have time to read the assignment.

1 Who are the victims of hate crime (name two)? 2
- _____
- _____

2 What is Merrick Garland's vision of society? 1
_____

3 What ways of eliminating hate crime are suggested (name two)? 2
- _____
- _____

4 What are the victims' reasons for not reporting hate crime? 2
- _____
- _____

5 What should be done as far as hate crime on social media is concerned? 2
- _____
- _____

6 How do some Asian-Americans react to hate crime (name one)? 1
_____

7 Why is it good that civil lawsuits are future-oriented? 2
- _____
- _____

Wortangaben:
NAACP: National Association for the Advancement of Colored People
to leverage: hier: sich etwas zu Nutze machen

Now listen to the recording again.

TEIL II: LESEN UND SCHREIBEN (AUFGABENSET 1)

Text — Call for global treaty to end production of 'virgin' plastic by 2040

Scientists say agreement must cover extraction of raw materials and pollution that blights seas and land

A binding global treaty is needed to phase out the production of "virgin" or new plastic by 2040, scientists have said. The solution to the blight of plastic pollution in the oceans and on land would be a worldwide agreement on limits and controls, they say in a special report in the journal *Science*.

Since the 1950s about 8 bn tonnes of plastic has been produced. The effects are everywhere. One of the report's authors, Nils Simon, said: "Plastics are ubiquitously found in increasing amounts worldwide, including in terrestrial environments and even inside the human body." The authors say the very properties that have made plastic an apparently essential modern material also make it a serious environmental threat.

Science senior editor Jesse Smith writes: "As for much new technology, their development and proliferation occurred with little consideration for their impacts, but now it's impossible to deny their dark side as we confront a rapidly growing plastic pollution problem. The time for preventing plastic pollution is long past – the time for changing the future of plastic in our world, however, is now."

The report calls for a new global treaty "to cover the entire lifecycle of plastics, from the extraction of the raw materials needed for its manufacture to its legacy pollution". The largest proportion of plastic waste comes from packaging materials (47 %), while textiles are responsible for 14 % and transport 6 %. Each year, 3 % of worldwide plastic waste ends up in the oceans; in 2010 that amounted to about 8 m tonnes of plastic.

Yet plastic production has continued to increase. In 2019, 368 m tonnes of newly made, or virgin, plastics were produced. By 2050, the production of new plastic from fossil fuels could consume 10–13 % of the remaining global carbon budget permissible to ensure temperatures rise to no more than 1.5 C above pre-industrial levels as required by the Paris climate agreement.

Simon calls for a binding global treaty to:
- Phase out the production of newly made or virgin plastic by 2040.
- Create a circular economy for plastic, incentivising reuse and refill and the elimination of substantial volumes of plastic pollution.
- Start a worldwide clean-up of plastic waste.

"Plastic pollution poses a considerable, even though not yet fully understood, threat to the environment, species, and habitats, as well as to cultural heritage," said Simon. Its social impacts include harm to human health, in particular among vulnerable communities, and it comes with substantial economic costs affecting especially regions depending on tourism.

"Addressing these challenges requires a transformative approach that facilitates measures to reduce production of virgin plastic materials and includes equitable steps toward a safe and circular economy for plastics."

Cleaning up the vast plastic waste footprint spread across the world requires the targeting of clogged waterways, drains and sewers in many developing countries that do not have rubbish collection services and where creating and boosting waste management services would be necessary. Producers of plastic would also be required to contribute to help fund clean-ups in some countries.

The impact of plastic pollution on the environment could trigger negative impacts which are irreversible, the report's authors warned. Matthew McLeod and his colleagues warned the plastic pollution of the oceans and land is at a rate which cannot be tackled by any cleanup, particularly when it affects remote areas. What is required is curtailing the emissions of plastic to the environment as rapidly and comprehensively as possible, they say.

A report by the NGO *Tearfund* last year revealed that just four companies, Coca-Cola, PepsiCo, Nestlé and Unilever were responsible for more than half a million tonnes of plastic pollution in six developing countries each year, enough to cover 83 football pitches every day. Report authors Sarah Kakadellis and Gloria Rosetto say plastic waste is poorly managed and that by 2050 as much as 12,000m tonnes of it is likely to have accumulated in landfills or the natural environment.

The scandals of plastic waste exports to developing countries were one example of the failure of mechanical recycling as an answer to the plastic pollution problem, said Kakadellis and Rosetto.

"Technology alone will not and cannot solve the plastic pollution crisis," said the authors. "No silver-bullet solution exists for the multifaceted nature of plastic pollution. The answer instead lies in a blend of approaches ... from a strong regulatory framework and the investment in effective waste collection and management infrastructure to the development of polymer chemistries, life-cycle design, and consumer behaviour."

(763 words)

Sandra Laville: Call for global treaty to end production of 'virgin' plastic by 2040, https://www.theguardian.com/environment/2021/jul/01/call-for-global-treaty-to-end-production-of-virgin-plastic-by-2040, © Guardian News & Media Ltd 2033

Aufgabe 1: Integrierte Aufgabe zum Leseverstehen

Summarize the dangers and threats of plastic production and plastic waste mentioned in the text. Use your <u>own</u> words.

Aufgabe 2: Textanalyse

Analyze the means the author uses to show the urgency of the plastic pollution problem.

Aufgabe 3: Erörterung/Stellungnahme

3.1 Textbezogen und materialbezogen

"Consumers are powerless when it comes to fighting plastic pollution."

Assess this statement also considering the information given in the graph and the text.

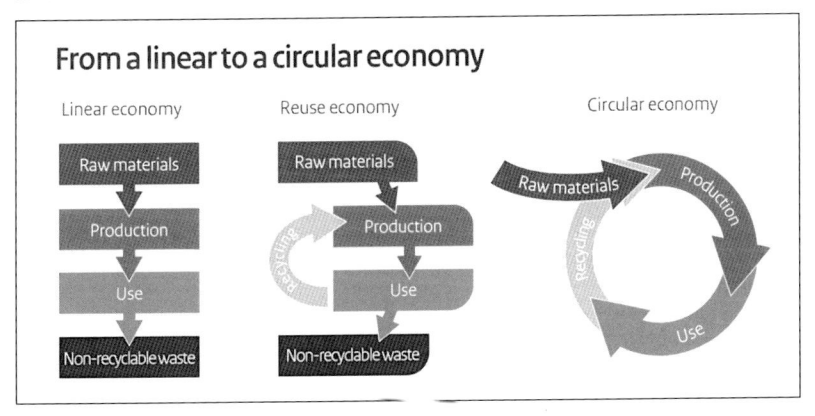

From a linear to a circular economy

Linear economy	Reuse economy	Circular economy
Raw materials → Production → Use → Non-recyclable waste	Raw materials → Production → Use → Non-recyclable waste (with Recycling loop)	Raw materials → Production → Use → Recycling (circular)

© *Government NL*

3.2 Themenbezogen

During the 2021 climate conference in Glasgow an agreement was signed by many countries to end deforestation by 2030.
You are taking part in a youth conference on climate action. At this conference, the effectiveness of this treaty is discussed. It becomes clear that individuals have to play a part in the fight to end deforestation.
Write a speech in which you appeal to the audience to support the fight against deforestation through their consumer behaviour.

TEIL II: LESEN UND SCHREIBEN (AUFGABENSET 2)

Text — America's gun obsession is rooted in slavery

Bodies are piling up all over the *Second Amendment* as two of America's pandemics converge. The "plague of gun violence" and the inability to mount an effective response, even in the wake of multiple mass shootings, is, unfortunately, rooted in the other pandemic gripping the United States: anti-Blackness and the sense that African Americans are a dangerous threat that can only be neutralized or stopped by a well-armed white citizenry.

For too long, the *Second Amendment* has been portrayed with a founding fathers aura swaddled in the stars and stripes. But "a well-regulated militia" wasn't, as the story goes, about how valiant and effective the militias were in repelling the British. George Washington was disgusted with their lack of fighting ability and the way the men would just cut and run from battling against a professional army. Nor was the militia reliable as a force to uphold the law. In Shays' Rebellion, bands of armed white men, who were in the state's militia, attacked the Massachusetts government because of foreclosures and debt seizures, demonstrating, again, how unreliable the militia were.

[...]

On the other hand, where the militia had been steadfast was in controlling the enslaved Black population. Access to guns for white people was essential for this function. In 1788, at the constitutional ratification convention in Virginia, a major source of contention was that the draft constitution had placed the training and arming of the states' militia under federal control. Virginians Patrick Henry and George Mason balked and raised the specter of a massive slave revolt left unchecked because Congress could not be trusted to summon the forces to protect the plantation owners. Mason warned that if and when Virginia's enslaved rose up (as they had before), whites would be left "defenseless". Patrick Henry explained that white plantation owners would be abandoned because "the north detests slavery". In short, Black people had to be subjugated and contained and state control of the militia was the way to do that.

The sheer brutality of human bondage [...] had created an overwhelming fear among whites and the enslaveds' capacity and desire for retribution. A series of revolts in the 1600s and 1700s terrified white residents and led to a slew of laws forbidding Black people from having any weapons, including guns. The militias' all-important role was to quash those revolts, especially if the uprising was widespread, as in the 1740 Stono Rebellion in South Carolina.

This function of the militias was so important during the War of Independence that governments such as that in South Carolina devoted the lion's share of their white manpower to the containment of the enslaved. As a result, the colony did not have enough white men to join the Continental Army and repel the British. [...] In other words, concerns about keeping enslaved Black people in check are the context and background to the *Second Amendment*.

The same holds true for today. In May 2000, NRA president Charlton Heston invoked the constitution and then asserted, as he held a 19th-century-era rifle over his head, that the only way that Al Gore and other liberals would take his gun would be "from my cold dead hands". That unyielding statement was a response to his people supposedly being under attack. [...]

Nearly two decades later the Colorado congresswoman Lauren Boebert [...] echoed that same defiance and fear [...]. Without weapons, she exclaimed in a fundraising ad, her overwhelmingly white constituency would be left defenseless against "gang members, drug runners and thugs", pejoratives that are often deployed as synonyms for African Americans.

Previously, Dana Loesch, NRA spokeswoman, had painted a similar picture of "them" screaming "racism", breaking windows, burnings cars, bullying and terrorizing "the law-abiding". [...]

Thus, the slaughters in Sandy Hook, the Pulse Club in Orlando, Mother Emanuel AME Church in Charleston and San Bernardino did not lead to any meaningful gun safety laws despite the staggering casualties. The rampant anti-Blackness that dominated Barack Obama's presidency helped to short-circuit[1] a tangible, legislative response. Instead, the fear of being left defenseless to a nation with a sizable Black population and Black leadership was palpable. Gun sales soared by 158 % as did the rise of anti-Black rightwing militias.

The Wisconsin senator Ron Johnson, who has an A rating from the NRA, sums it up. He didn't fear white insurrectionists who stormed the US Capitol, injured 140 police officers, built a gallows to "hang Mike Pence" and hunted for Nancy Pelosi; he would have been afraid, however, if it had been Black Lives Matter. Indeed, because that fear and the *Second Amendment* meant that Black lives don't matter. And whites and others caught in the crosshairs of mass shootings are the collateral damage and pay the price.

(792 words)

Carol Anderson: America's gun obsession is rooted in slavery, https://www.theguardian.com/commentisfree/ 2021/jun/04/america-gun-obsession-slavery, © Guardian News & Media Ltd 2033

Wortangabe:
1 to short-circuit: here: to prevent something from being successful

Aufgabe 1: Integrierte Aufgabe zum Leseverstehen

Summarize what reasons the author gives to show the connection between the Second Amendment and slavery as well as racial discrimination against Blacks.
Use your <u>own</u> words.

Aufgabe 2: Textanalyse

Analyze how the author tries to convince the reader of her critical attitude towards American gun culture.

Aufgabe 3: Erörterung/Stellungnahme

3.1 Textbezogen und materialbezogen

"The Wisconsin senator Ron Johnson [...] didn't fear white insurrectionists who stormed the US capitol [...]; he would have been afraid, however, if it had been Black Lives Matter." (ll. 60–63)
Comment on the statement from the text and include the message of the following cartoon.

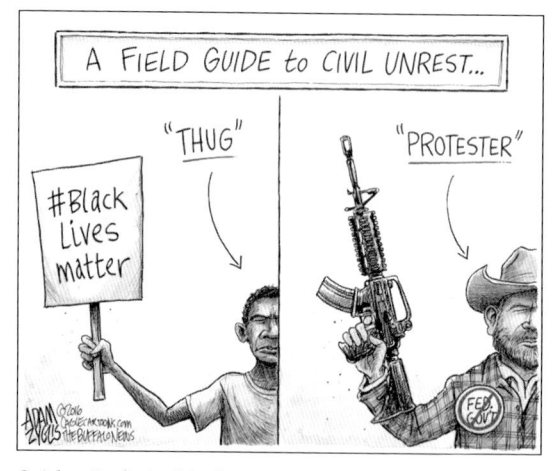

© Adam Zyglis/politicalcartoons.com

3.2 Themenbezogen

You are spending an exchange year at a high school in the USA. The news of recent school shootings has shocked the school community, and the topic of gun control is discussed hotly.
You are invited to write a contribution to the school blog (school magazine) in which you present the German perspective. Write a blog entry (magazine article) in which you assess the second amendment and US gun legislation from a German point of view.

TEIL III: KOMMUNIKATIONSPRÜFUNG

Tandemprüfung – Topic: Artificial Intelligence (Partner A)*

MONOLOGUE

You are a guest on a talk show that is discussing new developments in science and technology. Give a 5-minute presentation on Artificial Intelligence (AI) based on the following quotation, the cartoon and the graph.

In order to prepare your presentation you should consider the following tasks:
- explain and comment on the quotation
- describe and analyze the cartoon and refer it to the quotation
- describe and analyze the graph

Quotation

> "Society expects autonomous vehicles to be held to a higher standard than human drivers."
> (Professor Amnon Shashua)

Cartoon

Is that one of those cars that tells you when it needs maintenance?

Yeah, but I think it's a hypochondriac, or in partnership with my mechanic.

© Larry Lambert / Cartoonstock

MP-11

Graph**

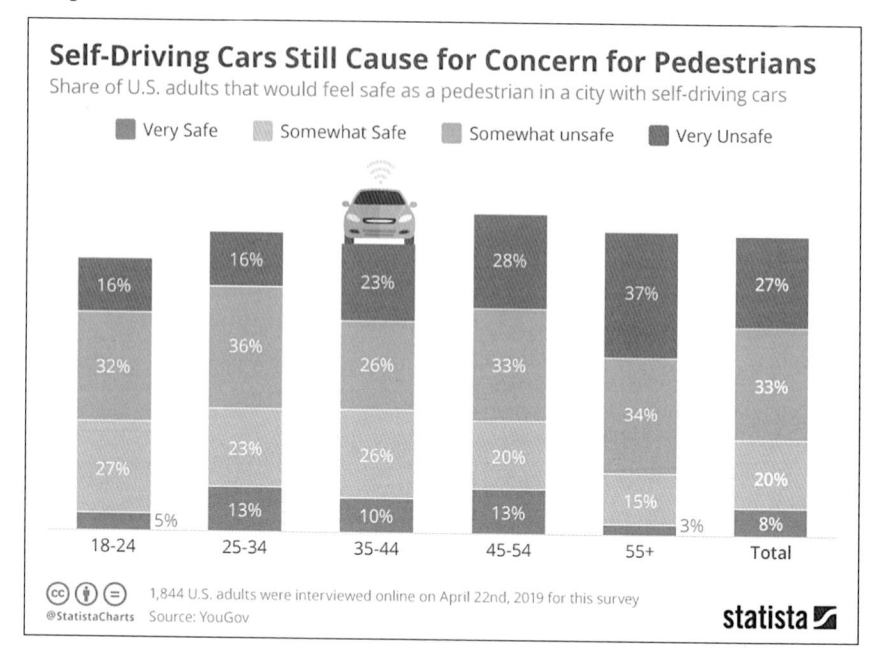

Self-Driving Cars Still Cause for Concern for Pedestrians
Share of U.S. adults that would feel safe as a pedestrian in a city with self-driving cars

Legend: Very Safe | Somewhat Safe | Somewhat unsafe | Very Unsafe

Age	Very Safe	Somewhat Safe	Somewhat unsafe	Very Unsafe
18-24	5%	27%	32%	16%
25-34	13%	23%	36%	16%
35-44	10%	26%	26%	23%
45-54	13%	20%	33%	28%
55+	3%	15%	34%	37%
Total	8%	20%	33%	27%

1,844 U.S. adults were interviewed online on April 22nd, 2019 for this survey
@StatistaCharts Source: YouGov

statista

DIALOGUE:
In the talk show, other topics are brought up.
Be prepared to discuss the pros and cons of self-driving cars and Artificial Intelligence (AI) in general.

* Hinweis: Dieser Teil der Tandemprüfung kann auch als Einzelprüfung absolviert werden
** Hinweis: Die Grafik steht Ihnen auf MyStark auch in Farbe zur Verfügung.

Tandemprüfung – Topic: Artificial Intelligence (Partner B)

MONOLOGUE

You are a guest on a talk show that is discussing new developments in science and technology. Give a 5-minute presentation on Artificial Intelligence (AI) based on the following quotation, the cartoon and the graph.

In order to prepare your presentation you should consider the following tasks:
- explain and comment on the quotation
- describe and analyze the cartoon and refer it to the quotation
- describe and analyze the graph

Quotation

> *"Autonomous vehicles are nowhere near as smart as they need to be. Safety features must be top priority."*
> (US senator Richard Blumenthal)

Cartoon

"Our smart car may be a little too smart. It says if we think it's going out in this rain, we're crazy!"

© Jerry King / Cartoonstock

Graph**

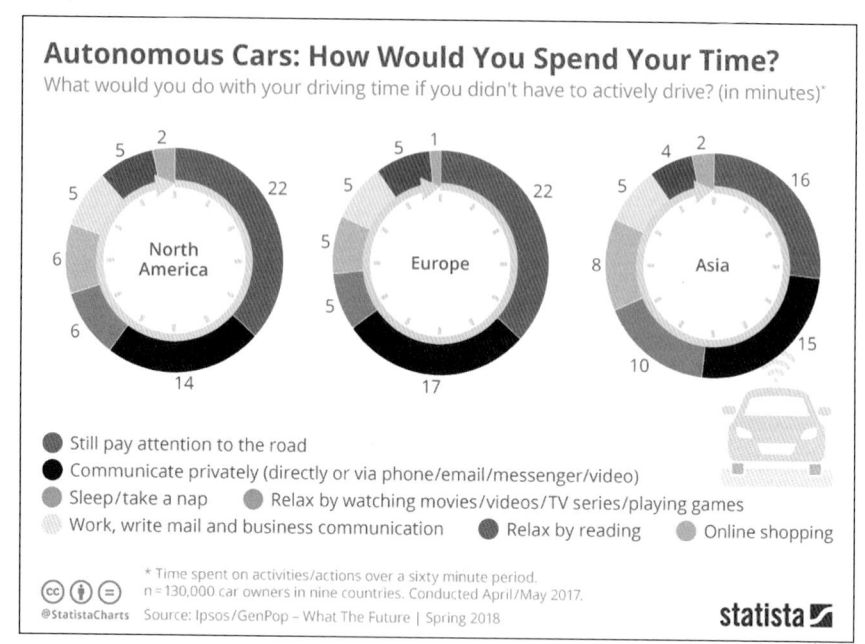

Autonomous Cars: How Would You Spend Your Time?
What would you do with your driving time if you didn't have to actively drive? (in minutes)*

North America: 5, 2, 22, 14, 6, 6, 5
Europe: 5, 1, 22, 17, 5, 5
Asia: 4, 2, 16, 15, 10, 8, 5

- Still pay attention to the road
- Communicate privately (directly or via phone/email/messenger/video)
- Sleep/take a nap
- Relax by watching movies/videos/TV series/playing games
- Work, write mail and business communication
- Relax by reading
- Online shopping

* Time spent on activities/actions over a sixty minute period.
n = 130,000 car owners in nine countries. Conducted April/May 2017.
@StatistaCharts Source: Ipsos/GenPop – What The Future | Spring 2018

statista

DIALOGUE
In the talk show, other topics are brought up.
Be prepared to discuss the pros and cons of self-driving cars and Artificial Intelligence (AI) in general.

** *Hinweis: Die Grafik steht Ihnen auf MyStark auch in Farbe zur Verfügung.*

Lösungen

🔊 TEIL I: HÖRVERSTEHEN

Transcript 1   3D printing

1. 3D printing is a whole collection of different manufacturing techniques, from having melted plastic extruded from a tiny nozzle or it can be a bed of metal powder that you shoot a high-powered laser at to melt the tiny, tiny grains of powder together. There's a whole bunch of different ways of doing it.

2. Rolls Royce right now, as I understand, is offering some 3D printed custom interiors to the cars so that you can design what you want your interior to look like. And, of course, on the gas savings, fuel savings, that's always a big issue.

3. I truly do believe that in the next decade the majority of Americans will have a 3D printer in their home. I truly believe that. They'll be printing out cups and plates and furniture and all these different things and some of those people will be printing out weapons with that. And I think that that's something that we should be talking about now.

4. There's whole businesses of people who want to have an exact image of themselves. Disney is offering some dolls that can be made with your child and you have the scan, you leave, you go ride the rides or whatever you do, then you come back, and you have a doll that looks just like your child as a princess.

5. Local workshops are clearly meeting an existing need all over the world where people are saying, we can make most of the tools and the products that we need locally. Or even more importantly, repair the stuff that we've bought from a mass producer of some kind but is otherwise hard to repair. And so, it's shifting the focus away from replacing mass produced products with locally mass-produced products and having a smaller number of things which we make and repair ourselves.

3D printing technology changes manufacturing processes from cars to kidneys, https://www.cbc.ca/radio/thecurrent/the-current-for-february-18-2016-1.3453054/feb-18-2016-episode-transcript-1.3454398#segment2

TIPP

You will hear five short excerpts from an interview about 3D printing. First, read through the task and the headings, which should be matched with the correct excerpts. You are only given a short amount of time for that, so a good knowledge of vocabulary will help as you won't have to look up words. Note down words you hear that you think are essential for understanding. You will have a short break between sets to look them up, but do not overestimate this time frame. The listening comprehension takes its complexity not only from the sophisticated level of English, but also from the speed in which you have to solve the tasks.

- **1 – B:** The heading "various processes" corresponds with the wording "collection of different manufacturing techniques" (l. 1) in the text. The examples given as well as "a whole bunch of different ways" (l. 4) also hint towards B.
- **2 – G:** Even if you do not know the meaning of "prestigious", you should know the word "personalisation" as it is similar to German. The key in the text lies in the phrase "design what you want your interior to look like" (l. 6). Mentioning the luxury brand Rolls Royce (l. 5), which is associated with a prestigious lifestyle, also adds to that solution.
- **3 – E:** At first you might think that the heading "empowered individuals" is correct, as the speaker mentions Americans printing out different things like cups or plates (ll. 9–11) in the future. However, they would also be able to print out weapons, which is something that should be talked about (ll. 11/12) and leads to the heading "dangerous perspective".
- **4 – A:** Finding the right solution can be tricky here, too. The audio mentions people who want to have an "exact image of themselves" (l. 13), so you might think that this is about "personalisation" (G), but the adjective "prestigious" would not fit here. It is also not "empowering" as mentioned in F. Therefore, only A is left: the printing of a doll is just a "trivial application", which means it is just a gimmick, something which is not really needed.
- **5 – F:** The speaker explains what "empowered individuals" are capable of doing with the help of 3D printing: "we can make most of the tools and the products that we need locally" or they can repair things themselves (ll. 18–20).

Speaker	1	2	3	4	5
Heading	B	G	E	A	F

Transcript 2   Auto industry

Ailsa Chang *(host)*: More than a dozen auto plants across North America are on pause as companies like General Motors and Ford deal with ongoing shortages of computer chips and other supplies. NPR's Camila Domonoske has been following the story and joins us now. Hey, Camila.

Camilla Domonoske *(byline)*: Hi, Ailsa.

Chang: So, what exactly is the problem facing these plants?

Domonoske: Well, the single biggest problem is a shortage of computer chips. The companies that make semiconductors just couldn't keep pace with how quickly demand for cars came back from pandemic lows. And there are a lot of computer chips in modern cars.

Chang: Yeah.

Domonoske: They're tucked in everything from engines to the seats. That's how they can tell if you're sitting in them. So, you now have plants shutting down for days to weeks. General Motors just announced two more plants that are going on pause. Ford has four down right now. And even plants that are still open – you know, most major automakers have had to cut production somewhere.

Chang: Wow. Wait. So is every automaker affected by this problem?

Domonoske: Well, right now Toyota and Honda are operating like normal in North America. The shortage is global, but it doesn't affect everyone equally at the same moment in time. You can kind of think back to last year when toilet paper suddenly disappeared from stores, right?

Chang: Right.

Domonoske: Everyone was facing a toilet paper shortage. But if you were down to your last roll at home, it was a really urgent situation. And if you had, like, a Costco pack that was mostly full, you were going to be fine for a little while. So, automakers – some of them are in different situations with their current stash of semiconductors than others. But two things – one, it might get worse for them as this stretches on, probably for months. But also, semiconductors are the biggest issue. But there are shortages of a lot of goods right now. Ann Wilson is with the Motor Equipment Manufacturers Association. That's a trade group for auto suppliers. Here's what she says.

Ann Wilson: We are seeing the greatest challenges to our supply chain that we have seen in decades, probably 20 or 30 years.

Domonoske: And by that, she means backlogs at ports, winter storms knocking out phone plants in Texas. There's a steel shortage, so that means even automakers who have enough computer chips on hand can still be hit in a crunch. Like, Honda is open now, but they had to close most North American factories just two weeks ago for all of these reasons.

Chang: Wow. Well, ultimately, Camila, what does all of this mean for the industry as a whole and for car buyers?

Domonoske: We're talking about a million cars delayed just from the computer chip problem, not even the other shortages. So, for carmakers, this is tens of billions of dollars in losses. For auto workers, they have temporary layoffs or cuts in their hours to deal with, reducing their take-home pay. There are ripple effects to other suppliers. When a plant goes dark, it affects every company that makes a part that feeds into that plant, right? And then on the shoppers, you know, if you're looking for a new car right now, they're going to be in shorter supply. And that will push prices up, and it means fewer options are available if you're looking for a particular configuration.

Chang: Right. Right. So how is the Biden administration responding to this so far?

Domonoske: Well, on Monday, there's going to be a meeting between the White House and a bunch of companies – Ford, General Motors, Stellantis, which was formerly known as Fiat Chrysler, as well as the semiconductor companies and tech companies to talk about what to do. It's clearly a top national concern for the administration. But things like investing in domestic supply chains – it's a long-term fix, not a quick solution.

Chang: That is NPR's Camila Domonoske. Thank you, Camila.
Domonoske: Thanks, Ailsa.

© 2021 National Public Radio, Inc. NPR News report "Auto Industry Continues To Struggle With Supply Chain Issues" was originally broadcast on NPR's All Things Considered on April 9, 2021, and is used with the permission of NPR. Any unauthorized duplication is strictly prohibited.

> **TIPP**
>
> The order of the tasks follows the order in the audio, and only one out of three alternatives is correct. However, the vocabulary is rather sophisticated, and so the correct answer is often hidden behind complex expressions. Before the first listening read the tasks carefully and mark expressions to look out for while listening. Also look up unknown words you might need to find the right solution. Moreover, be prepared to change your choice.
>
> 1 Although she mentions the pandemic, Ms Domonoske wants to say that the rising need for computer chips could not be met: "The companies that make semiconductors ["suppliers"] just couldn't keep pace with how quickly demand for cars came back from pandemic lows" (ll. 7–9).
> 2 Here, you need to listen out for the consequence for General Motors: "General Motors just announced two more plants that are going on pause." (l. 14), which eliminates "… close two factories forever" as well as "… lay off workers temporarily" because no workers are mentioned.
> 3 Toyota and Honda are only mentioned in the context of North America, where it is pointed out that they "are operating like normal" (ll. 18/19). Don't be distracted by "global" in the next sentence.
> 4 The overall content of the audio eliminates "… see more semiconductors on the market", which leaves alternatives a) and b). Ms Domonoske says: "[…] it might get worse for them as this stretches on, probably for months" (ll. 27/28), so a) is the correct solution. Although she mentions other problems and challenges later on, she says "semiconductors are the biggest issue" (l. 28).
> 5 Ms Domonoske gives several examples of challenges to the supply chain: "backlogs at ports", "winter storms" or "steel shortage" (ll. 34/35), which can also affect companies with no shortage of semi-conductors: "There's a steel shortage, so that means even automakers who have enough computer chips on hand can still be hit in a crunch." (ll. 35/36)
> 6 Listen closely to the part starting with "We're talking about a million cars delayed …" (l. 41), in which Ms Domonoske is talking about the financial consequences for car manufacturers: "So for carmakers, this is tens of billions of dollars in losses." (ll. 42/43), which is another way of saying "reduction in revenues".

7 In the text, the word "shoppers" is used for "buyers" (l. 46) and the consequences for them are elaborated on: "[…] if you're looking for a new car right now, they're going to be in shorter supply. And that will push prices up, and it means <u>fewer options are available</u> if you're looking for a particular configuration." (ll. 46–49)

8 Listen closely when President Biden is mentioned: "So how is the Biden administration responding to this so far?" (l. 50). Ms Domonoske then explains the strategy of his administration, saying "it's <u>a long-term fix,</u> not a quick solution." (ll. 55/56), which only points towards "will take some time".

1 There is a lack of computer chips in the car industry because its suppliers …
   b ✓ couldn't meet the rising need.

2 As a consequence General Motors had to …
   c ✓ stop production for some time.

3 At the moment, some major car manufacturers, like Honda and Toyota, are …
   b ✓ not affected in North America.

4 In the near future, car manufacturers will …
   a ✓ face a situation even worse.

5 If companies have enough semiconductors, they can …
   b ✓ still be affected seriously.

6 For the car manufacturers the delay in the production of cars means facing …
   c ✓ a reduction in revenues.

7 For potential car buyers it means …
   c ✓ limited choices.

8 For the Biden administration, fighting this crisis …
   a ✓ will take some time.

> **Transcript 3**   Attacks on minorities (FBI report)

Ari Shapiro *(host)*: Hate crimes in the U.S. are on the rise. The FBI reports that bias-motivated attacks are at their highest level in 12 years. NPR's Carrie Johnson is here to talk with us about the new data. And Carrie, what is the FBI saying about these incidents over the past year?

Carrie Johnson *(byline)*: The bureau says these crimes are up 6% year over year. And that increase is really notable, especially when it comes to hate crimes that are motivated by the race or ethnicity of the victims. The FBI says the Black community bore the brunt of these incidents in 2020. But Asian Americans and Pacific Islanders were also targets of a lot of hate. The attorney general, Merrick Garland, says there needs to be an urgent response. He says all people in this country should be able to live without fear of being attacked or harassed because of where they're from, what they look like, whom they love or how they worship.

Shapiro: So, what's the federal government doing to try to prevent these incidents and bring perpetrators to justice when they happen?

C Johnson: The Justice Department has been reaching out to communities. It's trying to make information about how to contact authorities available in languages other than English. And it's encouraging states and local jurisdictions to report these crimes to the FBI. Right now, these reports are voluntary. Experts say these crimes are severely underreported. Here's just one example. The Anti-Defamation League says more than 60 large jurisdictions nationwide reported no incidents – none at all – to the FBI last year. And they say that's really hard to believe. And all too often, there's another issue. Survivors of these crimes don't report to authorities because they lack trust in the police, or they worry about the consequences if they're undocumented people.

Shapiro: What are civil rights groups saying about this increase in hate crimes?

C Johnson: I reached Derrick Johnson, the president of the NAACP, a few hours ago. He says the Justice Department needs to bring more criminal prosecutions. He says it's about accountability.

Derrick Johnson: We must turn back the clock of the rise in racial hate crimes and hold people accountable and make sure social media platforms are not being leveraged to sow seeds of hate because when that happens, communities are put in danger. And in fact, our democracy is put in danger.

Shapiro: Carrie, you also mentioned that attacks have increased against Asian Americans. What are those groups saying?

C Johnson: Stop AAPI Hate, which advocates for Asian Americans and Pacific Islanders, says since March of 2020, they've received over 9,000 reports about verbal harassment, discrimination and even physical assaults targeting Asian Americans. Those reports are from all 50 states. And things have gotten so bad that some Asian Americans are going outside only after they put on a mask, sunglasses and a hat, a kind of protection from people who might want to harass them.

Manju Kulkarni co-founded Stop AAPI Hate. She says the Justice Department can also step up. She wants to see them file civil lawsuits over discrimination in hateful incidents in the workplace and in schools. She points out that those civil cases have a lower legal bar to succeed than criminal cases. Here's a little more from her.

Manju Kulkarni: When we look at civil prosecution, what one of the benefits is, is that it is forward-looking. You have an opportunity to change behavior. You have an opportunity for trainings, and it's really forward-facing.

Shapiro: All right. That is NPR's Carrie Johnson on the new hate crimes report from the FBI. Thank you very much, Carrie.

C Johnson: You're welcome.

© 2021 National Public Radio, Inc. NPR News report "Attacks On Minorities Are At Their Highest Level In 12 Years, FBI Reports" was originally broadcast on NPR's All Things Considered on September 2, 2021, and is used with the permission of NPR. Any unauthorized duplication is strictly prohibited.

TIPP

Here again, the order of the questions follows the order in the audio. This time you need to write down the solutions yourself. Often you only need to give one or two aspects out of several mentioned, and sometimes you can just write down what the speaker says. However, this requires an in-depth knowledge of vocabulary and the ability to distinguish between several native speakers talking. Pay attention to keywords the speakers use which can also be found in the tasks.

1 The solution can be found after Johnson speaks about hate crimes "that are motivated by the race or ethnicity of the victims" (ll. 6/7). She then lists "the black community" (l. 7), Asian Americans and Pacific Islanders (l. 8). Mentioning two out of three is enough for the task.

2 Listen closely when the name Merrick Garland is mentioned (cf. l. 9) as what comes next is the solution to the task: "He says all people in this country should be able to live without fear of being attacked or harassed because of where they're from, what they look like, whom they love or how they worship." (ll. 10–12). You can shorten your answer, for example by writing "all people living without fear of attacks or harassment".

3 The elimination of hate crimes (cf. task) and "try to prevent these incidents" (l. 13) are synonymous phrases here. The audio mentions several aspects of which you need to write down two: "reaching out to communities" (l. 15), "make information about how to contact authorities available in languages other than English" (ll. 16 f.) and "encouraging states and local jurisdictions to report these crimes to the FBI" (ll. 17/18).

4 Listen closely to what is said after "these crimes are severely underreported" (l. 18) as there will be reasons given for not reporting hate crimes: "they lack trust in the police, or they worry about the consequences if they're undocumented people" (ll. 23/24).

5 This can be a tricky task because "social media" is only mentioned once (ll. 29/30): "hold people accountable and make sure social media platforms are not being leveraged to sow seeds of hate"
6 The keyword "Asian Americans" in lines 33/34 signals that their situation will be described now and what some of them do to avoid being harassed: "put[ting] on a mask, sunglasses and a hat" (l. 39) when going outside.
7 Look out for the keyword "civil", which is mentioned several times: "civil lawsuits" (l. 42), "civil cases" (l. 43), "civil prosecution" (l. 45). "[F]orward looking" in line 46 then gives you the hint to the correct solution: "When we look at civil prosecution, what one of the benefits is, is that it is forward-looking. You have an opportunity to change behavior. You have an opportunity for trainings, and it's really forward-facing." (ll. 45–47)

1
- the Black community /
- Asian Americans /
- Pacific Islanders

2 all people living without fear of attacks or harassment /
a society in which people are not attacked or harassed

3
- reaching out to communities /
- information on how to contact authorities in other languages than English /
- encouraging states and local jurisdiction to report crimes to the FBI

4
- lack of trust in the police
- worry about consequences if they are undocumented

5
- people (using these platforms) should be held accountable
- make sure they are not used to sow seeds of hate / spread hate

6 they put on a mask, sunglasses and a hat to protect themselves

7
- opportunity to change behaviour
- opportunity for trainings

TEIL II: LESEN UND SCHREIBEN (AUFGABENSET 1)

Aufgabe 1: Integrierte Aufgabe zum Leseverstehen

> **TIPP**
>
> The assignment requires you to summarise the main points of the article, which means shortening the original text by concentrating on the aspects asked for: the dangers and threats of plastic pollution and plastic waste. Before you start writing, read the text carefully several times, highlighting the relevant parts. Mark passages which are not yet clear to you for later revision. Start your summary with an umbrella sentence including the title, author and topic of the original. Do not quote or copy from the text, use your own words, and avoid adding your opinion or interpretation. Use the present tense (simple form).
>
> introduction: title, author and source
>
> main part: the dangers and threats of plastic production and plastic waste
> - damage to the environment
> - danger to people's health, especially in poorer countries
> - export of plastic waste by industrial nations
> - massive plastic pollution also in oceans
> - production of plastic contributes to CO_2 emissions
>
> conclusion: only by a mix of measures can those dangers and threats be reduced

In her article in *The Guardian*, "Call for a global treaty to end production of 'virgin' plastic by 2040", the author, Sandra Laville, reports that scientists and researchers demand the production of new plastic to be stopped in view of the dangers and threats created by plastic pollution.	**introduction** reference to source and topic
The problem lies in the fact that plastic is produced in large quantities and can be found everywhere, having a damaging effect on the environment and the health of the population in poorer countries, in particular. These parts of the world, and above all the tourist centres, are hit especially hard because they lack proper waste management.	**main part** damage to environment and people's health
The problem is exacerbated by the industrialised nations, who export their plastic waste to developing countries and by multinational companies, who further contribute to plastic pollution by selling their products there.	made worse by plastic export
Plastic pollution is not only a major issue on land, but also at sea, where it endangers marine life. Furthermore, plastic contributes to the emission of CO_2 as it is made of fossil fuels, thus making it more difficult to reach the goals of the Paris climate agreement.	effect on the oceans contributing to CO_2 output

All in all, the dangers and threats caused by plastic pollution demonstrate that producing new, "virgin" plastic must be stopped and be replaced by an environmentally friendly mix of various measures.

(211 words)

conclusion
mix of measures

Aufgabe 2: Textanalyse

TIPP

This task requires a detailed linguistic analysis, showing what means regarding language and style the author uses to underline the urgency of solving the plastic pollution problem. In contrast to a summary, you should quote from the text here. Before you begin to write, read the text again carefully and highlight the linguistic devices used to convey the message. You can either bundle the devices or present them in chronological order.

introduction: author's intention

main part: linguistic devices
- words and phrases with negative connotations, setting a dark tone: "pollution that blights seas" (l. 1/2), "blight of plastic pollution" (l. 4), "serious environmental threat" (l. 11), "threat to the environment" (ll. 32/33), "dark side" (l. 14), "negative impacts which are irreversible" (ll. 45/46), "scandals of plastic waste exports" (l. 57) and "plastic pollution crisis" (l. 60)
- repetition of important aspects and words: "global", "impact"; "threat"
- vivid comparison: "enough to cover 83 football pitches every day" (ll. 53/54)
- references to scientists and scientific literature (l. 6) or by the NGO Tearfund (l. 51)
- use of figures, numbers, facts and statistics: virgin plastic produced since the 1950s (8 bn tonnes, cf. l. 7), tonnes of plastic waste in the oceans (8 m tonnes in 2010, cf. l. 21), percentage of packaging materials, textiles and transport responsible for plastic waste;
by the year 2050 plastic production will endanger the 1.5 C goal set by the Paris climate agreement (cf. ll. 22–26);
demands by scientist on how to avoid this scenario (ll. 27–30)

conclusion: linguistic devices emphasise urgency on tackling the issue

The author of the article discusses the issue of plastic pollution, which poses considerable hazards not only to our environment but also to people's health. From the way Sandra Laville presents her topic, it can be concluded that she considers solving the problem of plastic pollution to be an urgent task, which requires more effort than has been undertaken up to now. The writer tries to raise people's awareness of the issue and makes her viewpoint clear by using different stylistic and literary devices.

introduction
referring to the author's intention

Analysis of the vocabulary used in the article shows that the author frequently uses words and phrases associated with a negative meaning. She is thus setting a dark and warning tone to illustrate the dangers of excessive plastic production and inefficient plastic waste management. Expressions such as "pollution that blights seas" (ll. 1 f.), "blight of plastic pollution" (l. 4), "serious environmental threat" (l. 11), "threat to the environment" (ll. 33 f.), "impossible to deny their dark side" (l. 14), "negative impacts which are irreversible" (45/46), "scandals of plastic waste exports" (l. 58) and "plastic pollution crisis" (l. 60) emphasise the enormity and the menace of plastic pollution.

[**main part** / words and phrases with negative connotations]

Similarly, by repeating words with negative connotations such as "blight/to blight" and "threat" (both repeated twice) or words that show the huge effect plastic pollution has on people and the environment ("impact", repeated four times) the author further underlines her point that plastic pollution causes huge damage. In addition, she uses vivid comparisons to illustrate the dimension of plastic pollution, e. g. "enough to cover 83 football pitches every day" (ll. 54 f.), thus further emphasising the enormity of the problem.

[repetition and comparisons]

To give even more credibility to her appeal, Sandra Laville cites scientific sources such as reports in the journal *Science* or by the NGO *Tearfund*. She repeatedly cites plenty of numbers, facts and statistics, partly from those studies, to make the readers aware of the magnitude of the problem, e. g. by mentioning the tonnes of virgin plastic produced since the 1950s (8 bn tonnes, cf. l. 7), the tonnes of plastic waste in the oceans (8 m tonnes in 2010, cf. ll. 20 f.) or the percentage of packaging materials, textiles and transport responsible for plastic waste (cf. ll. 19 ff.). The author also cites studies, which say that by the year 2050 plastic production will even increase if nothing is done against the problem and that this will endanger the 1.5 C goal set by the Paris climate agreement (cf. ll. 22 ff.). However, there are also concrete demands presented by Nils Simon, a study author, that show how this scenario could be avoided if everyone pulled in the same direction (ll. 27 ff.).

[citation of scientific sources, numbers and statistics]

To conclude, the author uses language and style as well as statistics to effectively emphasise the urgency of tackling the plastic pollution problem.

[**conclusion**]

(476 words)

Aufgabe 3: Erörterung / Stellungnahme

3.1 Textbezogen und materialbezogen

> **TIPP**
>
> In this task, you are to assess the statement that "Consumers are powerless when it comes to fighting plastic pollution". This means you have to evaluate the claim and decide whether it is true or not. According to the assignment, you are to refer to the information in the article and the graph. In the text, experts explicitly mention the important role consumers play in the fight against plastic pollution (cf. ll. 64 f.). To further determine the validity of the statement, include information from the graph, which shows three models of dealing with plastic waste. Include background knowledge from the topics "resources, waste and recycling" in your argumentation.
>
> introduction: the problem of virgin plastic production
>
> transition: are consumers powerless?
> - graph: from a linear to a circular economy
>   - less waste in re-use economy
>   - almost no waste in circular economy
> - experts: consumers also play a role in this process:
>   - people need to get rid of throw-away-mentality
>   - raising awareness about the problem of plastic pollution
>   - combined consumer power: incentive for more sustainable packaging
>   - avoid plastic packaging, pressure on industry and politics
>
> conclusion: joint action needed from industry, politics and consumers

Sandra Laville's article discusses the problems connected with the production of virgin plastic, which has risen exponentially in the last decades and causes widespread harm to the environment, our waterways, oceans and the human body. So, what can individual consumers do when it comes to fighting plastic pollution? Are we powerless or can we make a difference?

First of all, the production of virgin plastic waste must be reduced. The graph shows three models of dealing with plastic from production to consumption and finally disposal: the linear economy, the re-use economy, and the circular economy. The linear economy is the most wasteful approach of dealing with plastic because nothing is recycled. The second model includes recycling, but there is still non-recyclable waste, and the third, or circular, economy represents the ideal solution: all plastic is recycled and used again, so no new, "virgin" plastic is produced.

margin notes:
introduction stating the problem

statement: transition to main part

main part graph: from a linear to a circular economy

To achieve this, according to experts, the problem of plastic pollution must be tackled on a global scale, including a variety of approaches, among them the participation of the consumers.

consumer behaviour part of the solution

Indeed, consumers must take responsibility, which means that they need to change their behaviour. Leaving the solution of the dilemma to industry, scientists, or legislators is not enough. Our current economic model takes a lot of energy and fossil resources, such as oil or gas, to make plastic products that are too precious to be used only once and then thrown away.

Only a small percentage of plastic is currently reused or recycled, with the largest part being incinerated, dumped in landfills, or the sea. People have adopted a throw-away mentality, disposing of plastic coffee cups, plastic bottles, and other plastic packaging without considering the consequences. To change this behaviour, people must be made aware of the problem, and about the role they can play in reaching a more sustainable economy. They need to realise that they are not powerless, that they can refuse to buy items made from plastic or buy less of them. If there is a critical mass of consumers who do this, producers will be encouraged to develop more sustainable products. Moreover, consumers must pressure politicians to act, for example, by imposing an extra tax on plastic products or requiring manufacturers to reduce packaging waste. Public campaigns have already shown positive results with plastic bags, single-use straws, plastic cutlery, and plates being banned. Fast-food chains have also started to phase out the use of plastic in their restaurants.

need to get rid of throw-away-mentality

raising awareness

consumer power

In conclusion, the statement that consumers cannot act against plastic pollution is fatalistic and false. We must not give up but make every effort to clean up our planet and thus make sure it still remains habitable for future generations. In a joint action, industry, legislators and consumers can work together towards a circular economy. So, we as consumers can help avoid the horror scenario that soon there will be more plastic in the ocean than fish.

conclusion
joint action needed

(488 words)

3.2 Themenbezogen

> **TIPP**
>
> When writing a speech, put yourself in the position of a speaker who addresses a larger audience. Depending on the context and the group you are addressing, choose a formal or less formal (casual) register (vocabulary, style). Also bear in mind the elements of a speech such as your greeting and closing off, for example "Ladies and Gentlemen" or "Hello, everybody ... / Dear friends ... / Good morning ... etc." to begin your talk, and "Thank you very much", "Thank you for your attention" or "Thanks for listening" to end it. To make your speech impressive, make sure to include rhetorical devices (e. g. addressing the audience personally, using rhetorical questions, etc.) and sequencing phrases (e. g. "first", "next up", "let me finish") to help listeners follow your arguments and train of thought. As with a comment, organise the speech into three parts: introduction, main part, conclusion.
>
> introduction
> - greeting; presenting the problem: causes of deforestation
>
> main part:
> - importance of the rainforests for our climate:
>   - trees absorb large amounts of carbon dioxide
>   - reasons for destruction of the rainforests
>   - logging and burning for business interests
>   - to meet the demand for meat, palm oil, biofuels and arable land
>   - to grow soy, sugar cane or maize, used for biofuels
>   - production of palm oil and meat
> - possible solutions:
>   - buy palm oil-free products
>   - reduce or give up meat consumption
>
> conclusion: appeal to act
> - use consumer power
> - help plant trees

Good morning everyone,

When was the last time you ate meat, perhaps a burger, sausage, steak, or a pork chop? Why do I ask? Meat production is one of the main causes of deforestation, taking place mainly in the rainforests, the lungs of our Earth. Other causes are biofuel and palm oil production. Today, I would like to talk to you about why deforestation has such an enormous impact on our climate and what *you* can do to help stop it. — **introduction** causes for deforestation

Rainforests are important because they absorb large amounts of carbon dioxide from the atmosphere, offsetting emissions from burning fossil fuels and preventing the Earth from heating up. The fact that governments agreed at the climate conference in Glasgow in 2021 to end deforestation by 2030 shows how much the view about the importance of the rainforests has changed. For decades, environmentalists have appealed to ban settlements and logging in the Amazon basin, in particular, because cutting down or burning primeval forests for economic use damages the climate. However, appeals to protect tropical rainforests have often been ignored, for example by right-wing Brazilian governments, and the deforestation rate has massively increased. And why? To pursue business interests and make profits. Tropical rainforests are cut down to meet the demand for meat, palm oil, biofuels and arable land.	**main part** important role of rainforests for the climate

economic use of the rainforests: business interests and profits |
| Let's talk about biofuels first. In order to meet the increasing demand for energy, forest areas are cleared to grow soy, sugar cane or maize, for example, which can be used as the basis for biofuels. Replacing fossil fuels to drive cars sounds great, doesn't it? But it comes at the cost of deforestation, which made conservationists campaign against the biofuel industry. However, the fact that it is more difficult and costly than expected to make large amounts of fuel from organic matter has been more effective to curb the production of biofuels than the protests against it. In contrast, the production of palm oil and meat is still a major cause for deforestation. And this is where all of us can and must act. So, how can we help protect our rainforests? | deforestation because of: biofuels

palm oil and meat |
Let's have a look at palm oil. This is a very popular commodity, used to produce a wide variety of items, from cookies to toothpaste and cosmetics. Over the years, vast areas of rainforest have been cut or burned down to make way for oil palm plantations, particularly in Indonesia and Malaysia – and this is where you come in. You can help the environment by buying products made of sustainable palm oil. Look for these products next time you shop – or, best of all, only buy palm oil-free products.	appeal to buy palm oil-free products or ones with sustainable palm oil
Next up: the meat industry. In the Amazon region, forests were cut down to create grazing land for cattle, in particular. We as consumers can support the fight against deforestation simply by reducing our consumption of meat. You are not required to stop eating meat altogether and turn vegetarian, although more and more people have taken this route. However, you can choose to eat less red meat or put meat on the table that has been produced on farms in your area.	appeal to reduce or give up meat consumption
With these examples, I'm trying to say that we cannot leave the solution to the problem of deforestation to governments or conser-	appeal to use consumer power

vationist groups: I'm convinced you and I must act too. We, as consumers, have the power to influence what and how much is produced. And, above all, how it is produced.

Let me finish by suggesting another way you can support the fight against deforestation: donate to charities that expand sustainable forests or that reforest areas which were rainforests once. It's clear from research that it will be impossible to control global warming if the rainforests are lost. Don't wait! Act now and do your part to stop deforestation.

Thank you for your attention. *(640 words)*

conclusion
last suggestion: help plant trees

final appeal to act

TEIL II: LESEN UND SCHREIBEN (AUFGABENSET 2)

Aufgabe 1: Integrierte Aufgabe zum Leseverstehen

> **TIPP**
>
> This part requires you to summarise the reasons the author gives to show why the Second Amendment and slavery as well as discrimination against Black people are connected. Use the simple present tense to write your text. Also pay attention to not quoting but paraphrasing the necessary information. All in all, your text should be neutral about the content of the original text. You can structure your text as follows:
>
> introduction: title, author and source
>
> main part:
> - the historical background of the Second Amendment
> - consequences today

In her article "America's gun obsession is rooted in slavery", published in *The Guardian* on 4 June 2021, Carol Anderson describes the connection between the Second Amendment, slavery and the discrimination of Black Americans.	**introduction:** reference to source and topic
According to the author, there is a common and deep-rooted belief in White American society that Black Americans are a threat – a belief stemming back to the days of slavery and the forming of militias. Militias and the access to guns by Whites were considered necessary in those days to keep the enslaved population under control. The fact that Black people were kept as slaves and were abused, led to a fear of vengeance among slave owners, with this fear being confirmed in the 17th and 18th century by a series of slave uprisings. This in turn led to the belief that Black people had to be kept in check with the help of the Second Amendment.	**main part:** historical background of the Second Amendment
Nowadays, however, there is another reason why the right to keep and bear arms on the grounds of the Second Amendment is being justified by many White Americans and the NRA, in particular: Black Americans are often indiscriminately linked by them to gang crimes, vandalism, damages to property, or drug dealing. Therefore, arming White people is seen as a legal way of defence against criminals, who in their eyes, are mostly Black. That is why White rioters and radicals, who stormed the Capitol, for example, are still considered to be less dangerous than Black Lives Matter activists.	consequences today

(249 words)

Aufgabe 2: Textanalyse

> **TIPP**
>
> Here, you need to concentrate on certain aspects of the text in detail and analyse how and why something was written, i. e. which function or effect a certain element of the text has. It is important that you prove your arguments by quoting words or phrases from the text. Also pay attention to whether you need to focus only on certain aspects. Here, you are supposed to highlight the means with which the author tries to convince the reader of her attitude towards American gun culture.
>
> It can help to mark linguistic devices in the text first. Next, take notes next to the highlighted parts about what effect these devices have. In your analysis you can either follow the chronological order of the text or bundle the stylistic devices and argumentative techniques. In the following solution, the latter has been done:
>
> introduction: author's intention
>
> main part:
> - dramatic language and imagery
>   - stark visualisation to make clear the extent of gun violence (e. g. ll. 3, 53, 55)
>   - metaphorically equating US gun culture and racism with lethal diseases (cf. ll. 2, 4)
> - historical examples to deconstruct the myth around the Second Amendment
>   - e. g. Shay's Rebellion (ll. 12/13)
>   - referring to authorities like George Washington (cf. ll. 10/11)
>   - showing that the militias' actual role was to keep the enslaved population in check (cf. ll. 19–26)
> - situation today: giving evidence that the Second Amendment is still used against the Black population
>   - depiction of White gun supporters (e. g. ll. 40–49)
>   - use of statistics to show correlation between racism and gun sales
>
> conclusion: the author makes a strong point that American gun culture is rooted in slavery

In her article, the author wants to convince the readers of her negative attitude towards American gun culture. She does this by employing various linguistic means.

First of all, she uses dramatic language to make clear the extent of gun violence as she speaks of "multiple mass shootings" (l. 3), animal-like "slaughters" (l. 53) and "staggering casualties" (l. 55), emphasising what horrible consequences the misuse of the Second Amendment has. The author also uses graphic imagery when speaking about the Second Amendment, beginning her text by picturing

introduction:
referring to the author's intention

main part:
dramatic language and imagery

"bodies [...] piling up all over the Second Amendment" (l. 1). Such stark visualisation gets the reader's attention immediately.

Carol Anderson even extends her use of imagery by employing a metaphor which equates the ongoing massive abuse of guns in the US with a lethal disease ("the 'plague of gun violence'", l. 2). At the root of this she sees racism towards African Americans and Black people in general. She compares this racism to a disease – here using the word "pandemic" (l. 4) – illustrating how she considers US gun bigotry and the inability to do something against it to be as devastating as a virus. metaphors

After illustrating the problem, the author deconstructs the myth around the Second Amendment by giving historical examples of the unreliability of the militias. In lines 8/9 she states that "a well-regulated militia" was not really about effectively fighting the British, "[nor was it] reliable as a force to uphold the law" (l. 12). Moreover, she mentions Shays' Rebellion when "bands of armed white men, who were in the state's militia, attacked the Massachusetts government" (ll. 12/13). To give her argument even more weight, the author also points out that George Washington thought the militias unfit to fight (cf. ll. 10/11), thus further supporting her stance that the right to bear arms as guaranteed in the Second Amendment was not based on the ability to help defend the country. historical examples to deconstruct the militia myth

In a next step, Anderson contrasts the militias' failure in effectively fighting a war with its relentlessness when it came to oppressing the slaves: "the militia had been steadfast [...] in controlling the enslaved Black population" (ll. 17/18). She again gives some historical evidence to support her view by, for example, mentioning politicians from the South demanding that the states should be in charge of training and arming the militias and not the federal government (cf. ll. 19–23), so that it would be possible for the slave holding states to crush slave revolts as happened, for example, in South Carolina in the 18th century (cf. ll. 28–33). Therefore, in the author's point of view, the right to bear arms (for White people) served no other purpose than to keep Black people in check (cf. ll. 26/27, ll. 38/39). historical examples of the militias' actual role

After her digression on history, the author focuses on the present situation, about which she says that "the same holds true for today" (l. 40). She illustrates her argument by depicting gun supporters and NRA members to make the reader aware that these are people with a stubborn and inhumane mindset. For example, she cites actor Charlton Heston, who held a rifle over his head and shouted that the only way one could take this gun from him was from his "cold dead hands" (cf. ll. 40–43), or congresswoman Lauren Boebert, who indirectly insulted Black Americans as criminals who threaten White Americans (cf. ll. 45–48) thus revealing the true mentality of the people the author sees as responsible for America's gun obsession. situation today: depiction of gun supporters

To further support her argument, the author also employs statistics that show a correlation between gun sales, which rose by 158 %, and the increase of anti-Black right-wing militias (cf. ll. 58/59), showing that the Second Amendment is still used to arm White Americans against an alleged "Black threat".

statistics: correlation between racism and gun sales

To sum up, the author uses dramatic language and imagery, historical examples, citations and statistics to convince the reader that American gun culture is rooted in slavery and continues to be.

conclusion

(679 words)

Aufgabe 3: Erörterung/Stellungnahme

3.1 Textbezogen und materialbezogen

> **TIPP**
>
> Here, you are supposed to comment on the statement from the text while also including the message of the cartoon given. It requires you to think outside the box and to also use your background knowledge. At the end of your text, you should give your own opinion. You can start by explaining the quote and using it as a starting point for your thoughts in the main part. Then, give reasons for your opinion. Use connectives whenever possible. Before you start writing, however, read the statement from the text carefully and decide on how you would interpret it. Your comment should be written in the simple present.
>
> introduction: explanation of the statement; thesis: opinion based on individual perception and prejudice
>
> main part:
> - definition of who is considered an insurrectionist differs
>   - Black Lives Matter: legal protest movement
>   - storm on the Capitol: dismissed by many Whites as being not as dangerous as Black Lives Matter movement: cartoon illustrates this attitude
> - reasons for different perceptions
>   - personal, cultural and racial background
>   - historical background of the Second Amendment
>
> conclusion: being aware of these reasons may prevent prejudice and intolerance.

In her text "America's gun obsession is rooted in slavery", Carol Anderson indirectly quotes senator Ron Johnson, who feared Black Lives Matter more than the white insurrectionists storming the US capitol on 6 January 2021. Black Lives Matter is a movement that gained national drive after acts of police brutality led to the deaths

introduction: explanation of the statement and transition to main part

of several Black US citizens. In most cases, the police officers involved were not prosecuted, thus sparking the protest even more. The statement shows that Black Lives Matter is seen as a threat by many Whites people, in this case a senator from Wisconsin. In the following essay, it will be shown that a controversial opinion like his is based on individual perception and prejudice.

An insurrectionist can be described as someone who tries to violently overthrow a government. Black Lives Matter is a political and social protest movement whose aim is not to overthrow a rightfully elected government, so from a legal point of view, it is the people who stormed the Capitol who are insurrectionists. Senator Johnson's attitude, however, shows that even acts of violence like the attack on the Capitol are not seen as an insurrectionary act by him nor as dangerous as Black people marching in peaceful protest. [main part — subjective definition of "insurrectionist"]

The senator's view, and that of many Whites in the US, is also depicted in the cartoon, in which a peaceful Black Black Lives Matter protester is offensively labelled "thug", whereas a clearly aggressive White with a machine gun in his hand and an anti-federal-government-button on his shirt is labelled with the neutral or even positive term "protester". [relation to the cartoon]

Whether people see a certain act as positive or negative depends rather on one's personal as well as cultural and racial background than on objective and legal considerations. If you grew up believing that only White people are decent and well-behaving people while you see Black people in a negative way, you will consider the people storming the Capitol as protesters rather than insurrectionists who want to overthrow a rightful government. [reasons for different perceptions]

It is important to see that these different perceptions have always had an impact on US society and the fight for equal opportunities for all. Racism and inequality have always been part of American history, although the US pledge of allegiance states "liberty and justice for all", with Black people, however, being the ones who have been denied that for a long time. There is a deep-rooted fear of White people, which goes back to the days of slavery, that Blacks may revolt against their White suppressors, so the militias mentioned in the Second Amendment were also installed to protect White landowners from Black rebellions. This leads to the situation we are still facing today: violence by Whites is mostly seen as an act of defence, whereas Black people fighting for their rights are seen as a threat. [historical background]

Thus, it can be concluded that our views are a result of different factors which make up individual perception. It is important to be aware of that in order not to give way to prejudice or intolerance. [conclusion]

(505 words)

3.2 Themenbezogen

> **TIPP**
>
> In this task you need to write an article for a school magazine or a school blog, which means that you as a student write to other students, so your language can be colloquial, but it should not be too informal or even slangy. Be friendly and respectful and write in the first person singular. You might want to include examples or stories from your own experience, too. By using stylistic devices you can make your article or blog vivid and interesting. The following criteria should be met:
> – Start with an interesting headline.
> – Put the topic you are writing about in the first paragraph.
> – Continue with further details, explanations, etc. in the following paragraphs.
> – End with a conclusion or one final thought. Maybe you want to invite your readers to join a discussion outside the blog post.

In the hands of a pandemic – the plague of gun violence **A German's view on the right to bear arms**	headline
The Second Amendment is clear: "A well regulated Militia, being necessary to the security of a free State, the right of the people to keep and bear Arms, shall not be infringed." But does that mean that keeping and bearing arms cannot be controlled? While in most US states there is hardly any restriction to this fundamental "right of the people", the country is leading in terms of gun violence and mass shootings. Germany, where I come from, also allows people to keep arms, and there have been shootings as well. However, the right to bear arms is much more restricted than in the US. I think, the difference in legislation is one of the reasons why there is less gun violence in Germany.	introduction difference in gun legislation between US and Germany
To begin with, if you want to have a weapon in Germany, you must apply for it. You need to prove that a weapon is essential for your hobby or job, and people younger than 25 need a medical record that states their physical and mental health. Gun ownership is therefore restricted to a relatively small number of people like hunters, target shooters, or security workers. Even then, you need to register your weapon and you are not allowed to carry it in the street, for which special permission is necessary. In the US, on the other hand, you can get guns almost as easily as milk, eggs and sweets! Background checks? Not really a serious hindrance.	main part gun ownership in Germany: stricter laws US: easy availability of guns
This situation will not change because lobbyism of the NRA is fierce. I would even go so far as to use the term propaganda, which promotes the fear of an all-time threat which makes it essential for	fierce lobbyism

every citizen to arm themselves, teaching even children to handle weapons and pistols. Just like a plague, weapons are everywhere.

For me, it is therefore questionable to uphold the Second Amendment. There is no "militia" anymore. What for do you have a national guard, trained police and experienced military? A sovereign state with a constitutional government does not need to rely on amateur shooters for its security! And finally, Jefferson, Franklin and others could not have known that almost everyone would be able to buy weapons at Walmart over 200 years later. — Second Amendment: does it still make sense?

So, I strongly believe that changing legislation is the key to dealing with US gun violence. Although laws do not make gun violence impossible and, above all, need to be enforced, stricter gun laws can make a country a safer place to live. — **conclusion** key to less gun violence: stricter legislation

Join us for discussion next Thursday in the cafeteria. I'd love to hear your opinion!

(399 words)

TEIL III: KOMMUNIKATIONSPRÜFUNG

Tandemprüfung – Topic: Artificial Intelligence (Partner A)

TIPP

For this part of the exam you will be provided with information about your communication situation (you are a guest on a talk show) and additional material, including a quotation, a cartoon and a graph. You are expected to speak freely for about five minutes. Follow the tasks closely which are listed on your exam paper. Don't wait for the teacher to respond or ask you a question.

- explain the quotation and comment on it: people tend to distrust autonomous vehicles
- description and analysis of the cartoon: owner of self-driving car and friend in conversation, sarcastic answer: car requires more services than needed
  - message: self-driving cars will outsmart humans
  - relation to quotation: cartoonist shares sceptical view expressed in quotation
- description and analysis of the graph: illustrates safety concerns of pedestrians towards self-driving cars, overall result: most people still have reservations against self-driving cars as road-users

MONOLOGUE

Beispiellösung:

The topic today is Artificial Intelligence (AI) and self-driving cars, in particular, which don't need a human being as a driver. I'll start with the quote of a professor, Amnon Shashua. The gist of what he says is that people only trust autonomous vehicles if using them is safer than sitting in a car with a human driver. quotation: explanation and comment

Next, there is a cartoon that shows two men standing in front of a self-driving car. The man on the right seems to be the owner of the vehicle, the other one maybe his friend. The friend asks the car owner whether his clever car tells him when it needs maintenance. The owner's sarcastic answer is he thinks his car is a hypochondriac or has a partnership with the garage, attributing human-like features to it. The self-driving car in the cartoon is showing concerns about its "health", thus requiring more servicing than necessary, and making the owner suspect the vehicle to help increase the mechanic's business. The cartoonist suggests that cars might one day turn out to be smarter than humans, and hard to control. This may still be a humorous exaggeration, but it could be seen as a warning of what could happen if machines develop a mind of their own. In this way, the cartoon: description and analysis

relation to the quotation

cartoon shares the skeptical message Professor Shashua's statement conveys as you do not know what "intelligent" machines, for example self-driving cars, are capable of doing.

The graph "Self-Driving Cars Still Cause for Concern for Pedestrians" shows how safe or unsafe U.S. adults of various age groups would feel in a city with self-driving cars. Five columns represent the different age groups: 18–24, 25–34, 35–44, 45–54 and 50+. They show the percentage of pedestrians who would feel "very safe", "somewhat safe", "somewhat unsafe" or "very unsafe". The sixth column gives the total percentage of respondents. The results reveal that the pedestrians who feel "very unsafe" are mostly 55 years and older. People younger than that tend to be less worried, with pedestrians who would feel "very safe" being mainly in the groups 25–34 and 45–54. Looking at the total numbers, it becomes clear that only 28% of adults would feel safe or somewhat safe, whereas the overwhelming rest had more or less grave doubts about their safety. Overall, the survey indicates that most people still have reservations about self-driving cars as road-users.

graph: description and analysis

> **TIPP**
>
> In the following, second part of the exam, you will talk with your teacher and/or your partner about the topic of self-driving cars. In this part, you are given no material, but you have to draw on your own knowledge of AI and self-driving cars. Show that you are familiar with the pros and cons of AI technology and that you are also able to hold a proper conversation. Pay attention to what your partner is saying, do not interrupt, stay on topic, and ask for clarification if in doubt.

DIALOGUE

Pros and cons of self-driving cars and Artificial Intelligence (AI) in general:

Beispiele:

pros
- increase of road safety: no human errors or misbehaviour
- can also be used by people who cannot drive or are handicapped
- time for other activities while on the road: e. g. sleeping, reading, phoning
- smooth traffic flow, including speed limit: cars running more efficiently: e. g. no excessive speeding, no sudden breaking and accelerating: better for the climate

cons
- safety concerns:
  – malfunction of hardware or software can lead to accidents
  – criminals may hack into the system if sensitive data and information is not protected

- passengers at the mercy of technology: no chance to intervene if technology fails?
- professional drivers becoming superfluous

Tandemprüfung – Topic: Artificial Intelligence (Partner B)

TIPP

For this part of the exam you will be provided with information about your communication situation (you are a guest on a talk show) and additional material, including a quotation, a cartoon and a graph. You are expected to speak freely for about five minutes. Follow the tasks closely which are listed on your exam paper. Don't wait for the teacher to respond or ask you a question.

- explain the quotation and comment on it: doubts about superiority of self-driving vehicles
- description and analysis of the cartoon: couple in self-driving car which refuses to go out in the rain
  - message: self-driving cars can develop their own mind
  - relation to quotation: self-driving cars may outsmart humans, but could act unpredictably
- description and analysis of the graph: study on how people would spend their time in a self-driving car, overall result: people on all continents would still concentrate on the traffic most of the time, but Asians seem to be more relaxed

MONOLOGUE

Beispiellösung:

The topic of Artificial Intelligence (AI) and self-driving cars, which don't need a human driver, can be introduced with a quote by a US senator, who doubts the superiority and reliability of autonomous vehicles. In his view, it is most important that autonomous vehicles are safe. *quotation: explanation and comment*

The following cartoon shows a scene in a garage. A couple are sitting in their self-driving car and are about to set out on a ride. The garage door is open, and one can see that it is raining heavily outside. In the caption, the driver says to his partner that he thinks their smart car may be a little too smart because it refuses to go out into the rain. Judging from their facial expressions, the woman is taken aback and surprised, while the man is angry. The self-driving car seems to have developed a mind of its own. It rebels against its owner, and, like an obstinate child, refuses to go out in the rain for fear of getting soaking wet. Here, the car acts like a human being. The cartoonist shows that the car has won the upper hand, with the role of "master" and "servant" being reversed. The machine rules over man. *cartoon: description and analysis*

Comparing the cartoon to the US senator's statement, the self-driving car in the cartoon has become smarter as need be by developing a mind of its own. The safety aspect, which the politician emphasises, is not addressed in the cartoon, but a human-like car could also stand in the way of safety by acting unpredictably.

In a study, researchers wanted to find out how people would spend their time in a car if driving was done autonomously. The graph displays the results of people's answers in North America, Europe and Asia. On the whole, drivers in all of the continents examined would still spend most of their time paying attention to the road. However, American and European "drivers" still seem more concerned about safety than Asians because they would spend six minutes more on concentration on the traffic (22 min. to 16 min.). In second place is "communicating privately" for which drivers in North America, Europe and Asia would reserve about 14–17 minutes. In all three continents, people in autonomous cars would dedicate the least amount of time to online shopping (1–2 min.). In contrast to Americans and Europeans, however, Asians would spend twice as much time sleeping or having a nap while the car is driving autonomously (10 minutes to 5 and 6 min. respectively). Similarly, Asians would spend more time watching movies or TV (8 min. compared to 5 and 6 min.). Although people in all continents would still focus on the traffic most of the time when sitting in an autonomous car, Asians seem more relaxed, which could mean they put greater trust in autonomous vehicles than Americans or Europeans.

relation to the quotation

graph: description and analysis

DIALOGUE
see Partner A

Baden-Württemberg • Abiturprüfung 2021
Berufliches Gymnasium • Englisch

TEIL I: LISTENING COMPREHENSION   10 VP

You will hear each recording twice. After each listening, you will have time to complete your answers.

Task 1: Film reviews   6 BE

You will hear excerpts from six film reviews. Match each review (1 to 6) with one of the descriptions (A to G). For each review there is only one correct description. There is one more description than you need.
You now have 45 seconds to read the assignment.

	Descriptions
A	Encounters between rich and poor
B	The abuse of power and its cover-up
C	A biography shaped by illegal activities
D	A comparison of stereotypical lifestyles
E	A movie star's lang history of drug-addiction
F	The rise and fall of a politician in a corrupt world
G	A sports contest as a metaphor for the film industry

Film review	1	2	3	4	5	6
Description						

Now listen to the recording again.

Task 2: The History of Jim Crow and Blackface   10 BE

You will hear a podcast about the history of Jim Crow and its connection to the current debate about blackface. While listening, answer the questions below. You need not write complete sentences.
You now have one minute to read the assignment.

1	According to the speaker, what did the Jim Crow laws embody?	• *hate* •
2	What has recently led to a new public discussion about Jim Crow?	
3	What was the purpose of the Jim Crow impersonations in the past?	
4	What was typical of the Jim Crow stage performance? (Name **two** aspects).	• •
5	Where did Thomas D. Rice get his inspiration for the Jim Crow character from?	
6	What was the consequence of Rice's performance?	
7	According to Daryl Davies, what does the perception of blackface depend on?	
8	Which positive example of the use of blackface does Daryl Davies mention?	
9	Which incident led to TV host Megyn Kelly losing her job?	

Annotations
buffoon: someone who does silly and amusing things
vernacular: form of language spoken by a particular group of people

Now listen to the recording again.

Task 3: The Mindful Chef 8 BE

You will hear an interview about the rise of the online service *The Mindful Chef*. While listening, tick (✓) the correct answer (a, b, c or d). There is only one correct answer. You now have two minutes to read the assignment.

1 *The Mindful Chef* is an online recipe box delivery service that has …
   a ☐ moved to London recently.
   b ☐ been operating since 2001.
   c ☐ received a prestigious prize.
   d ☐ run counter to recent trends.

2 When the partners started their business, they …
   a ☐ were desperate for money.
   b ☐ were disillusioned with their jobs.
   c ☐ had been toying with the idea for a while.
   d ☐ had been persuaded by business friends.

3 According to Giles Humphries, this new start would allow them to …
   a ☐ grow closer to their friends.
   b ☐ make the most of their skills.
   c ☐ feel more satisfied in their job.
   d ☐ use their working time more flexibly.

4 Looking back, Humphries says that coming home late from work they …
   a ☐ had no idea what to eat.
   b ☐ did not feel stressed at all.
   c ☐ were too exhausted to go shopping.
   d ☐ were unable to go to their gym classes.

5 In the summer of 2014 Humphries observed Devon fishermen …
   a ☐ preparing traditional sea food.
   b ☐ offering their catch door-to-door.
   c ☐ changing the natural food chain.
   d ☐ using modern media to sell their fish.

6 At the beginning of their business, Humphries and his co-founders …
- **a** ☐ did the packaging themselves.
- **b** ☐ used cargo bikes to avoid traffic jams.
- **c** ☐ built storage facilities for their ingredients.
- **d** ☐ suffered from constantly working night shifts.

7 In their marketing strategy, they relied on …
- **a** ☐ UK-wide advertising.
- **b** ☐ pictures shown on social media.
- **c** ☐ flyers distributed during deliveries.
- **d** ☐ cooperation with local newspapers.

8 Success came after Humphries and his co-founders …
- **a** ☐ automated the packaging.
- **b** ☐ employed a public relations team.
- **c** ☐ hit the half-a-million pounds mark.
- **d** ☐ tackled initial problems successfully.

Now listen to the recording again.

Lösungen

TEIL I: LISTENING COMPREHENSION

Transcript 1   Film reviews

Snippet/film 1: It's about, you know, Frank Sheeran, the, the main character, who is a real man and him looking back at his life of crime and it says so much, I think, about the futility of crime and just what happens when you are sort of the middleman doing everyone's dirty work and there is no one left to look after you at the end and your family has turned on you and, you know, you have just countless numbers of people's blood on your hands.

Snippet/film 2: I know it can also seem a little obvious in some ways, I felt it was beautiful to see it kind of work through in this meadow way in this film, which why using the racing world as its, as its subject, this really is, it seems to me, about the kind of very, very, working of the movie business now, especially when you deal with big studios.

Snippet/film 3: This is a movie that is made in South Korea, erm, and has had a level of impact that Korean films typically do not in the United States and in other countries and this is a movie that puts the haves and have-nots front and center, but in ways that are really subversive and that are not banal or kind of expected. I mean this is a really surprising movie. I think it's the best of a number of movies that have taken on class this year.

Snippet/film 4: I felt, this movie I had the most fun with it and did a lot with it. Because that's one of the central questions as one character wants to move to L.A. and the other has wanted to stay in New York, and so there is theater and there's TV and it's, you know, people put on sunglasses as soon as they are in L.A. and then the Brooklyn people all have, like, lattes. And this is an interesting way that it plays with that.

Snippet/film 5: But it's the rigorous understatement of the assistant that makes it so powerful in its vision of how easily the Harvey Weinsteins of the world could exploit their absolute authority for years with little fear of consequence. Moment by moment it pulls us into a world where predatory behavior is concealed behind closed doors and the silence of a hushed workplace becomes its own kind of complicity.

Snippet/film 6: "Judy" begins with one of several flashbacks to the teenage Garland on the set of "The Wizard of Oz" showing us how the industry created and destroyed her in the same breath. Her body and image are ruthlessly controlled by the powerful MGM studio head, Louis B. Mayer, who puts her on a strict diet and gives her barbiturates and amphetamines setting in motion the substance abuse problem that she will struggle with for the rest of her life.

TIPP

In this task you will hear short fragments or snippets of film reviews. These fragments have to be matched with the respective descriptions. In order to match the fragments and definitions correctly, it is essential for you to find signal words and know their synonyms. That is why you should learn word families or lexical fields with umbrella terms. This will enable you to find the necessary information fast.

- **1 – C:** There are some signal words in the description (C) which show you that the film is a biography and that it is about illegal activities: in the film review the name of the protagonist is mentioned (which may suggest a biographical film), but expressions like "life of crime" (l. 2), "futility of crime" (l. 3), "dirty work" (l. 4) and "people's blood on your hands" (ll. 5 f.) also indicate that the film is about illegal activities. That is why E and F cannot match as the definition is about more than corruption or drug abuse.
- **2 – G:** In the audio, "racing world" (l. 9) and "big studios" (l. 10 f.) are mentioned, which belong to the same word families as the terms "sports contest" and "film industry" in the description (G).
- **3 – A:** The synonyms here are "rich and poor" (in description A) and "haves and have-nots" in the audio fragment (l. 14).
- **4 – D:** Here you need to notice that the audio snippet is built as a comparison (see description): the speaker talks about "one character … and the other", "theatre … and TV", "people … in LA, and then the Brooklyn people" (ll. 19 ff.). There are also "stereotypical lifestyles" mentioned: "people put on sunglasses … in L.A." and "Brooklyn people all have, like, lattes" (ll. 21 f.).
- **5 – B:** General knowledge can be of help here: The audio names Harvey Weinstein, who exploited his position as a movie producer and was charged with sexual abuse, and the definition also mentions an "abuse of power". There are also synonyms for "abuse of power" and "its cover-up" in the audio: "exploit their absolute authority" (l. 24 f.) and "predatory behaviour", which is "concealed behind closed doors" (l. 26), as well as "silence" and "complicity" (l. 27). Note that "cover-up" is different from "corruption", which is why F is not an option here.
- **6 – E:** General knowledge can help you here too: the audio mentions the actress Judy Garland, who played Dorothy in the movie "The Wizard of Oz". This points to definition E, which refers to a "movie star". The term "drug addiction" in the definition corresponds to the mentioning of "barbiturates and amphetamines" in the audio (l. 31 f.) as well as "substance abuse problem" (l. 32).

Film review	1	2	3	4	5	6
Description	C	G	A	D	B	E

Transcript 2 — The History of Jim Crow and Blackface

Jim Crow, you've no doubt heard this name before. It's a name that has stood for hate and for the laws, the Jim Crow laws, that made racial segregation in the South legal until the Civil Rights Movement in the 1960s. Now that ugly name has reemerged in the American vernacular thanks to the recent political scandals unfolding in Virginia, where both the governor and attorney general have admitted to wearing blackface in their past. "I took responsibility for content that appeared on my page in the Eastern Virginia Medical School yearbook. That was clearly racist and offensive".

So, what's the connection between Jim Crow and blackface? Well back in the 1830s, Jim Crow wasn't yet a symbol of inequality. He was a fictional character in minstrel shows who, to entertain his audiences, danced like a buffoon and spoke with an exaggerated imitation of Black slave vernacular. Intended to be comedic minstrel shows were first performed in New York with White actors who wore tattered clothing and used shoe polish to blacken their faces, according to the Smithsonian's National Museum of African American History and Culture. While society now considers donning blackface as clearly racist, according to historians, the practice, especially on stage, was celebrated by Whites in the South following the Civil War.

Who was behind Jim Crow? A man, a White man, named Thomas Dartmouth Rice. Rice was born in 1808 in New York. As a teenager he began travelling the country as an actor. According to a University of South Florida history of minstrel shows, Rice was a dancer and a singer who drew from his observations of Blacks in the South to create an extremely exaggerated and stereotypical Black buffoon. While he wasn't the first White comic to perform in blackface, Rice was the most popular of his time and as a result the character of Jim Crow spread, becoming a common stage persona. The big lips, the lack of education, the poor clothing, that's how Daryl Davis, a Black blues musician who has studied these shows described these minstrel characters in an interview.

It wasn't about trying to look Black, he said, but trying to look Black in a way that portrays Blacks negatively. Davis has long argued that context is key when judging the use of blackface; in the 1900s, for example, White artists such as Al Jolson painted their faces as they performed ragtime and blues music pioneered by African Americans. Davis credits Jolson with spreading Black music to White audiences and advocating for Black artists. In the internet age, social media has fueled furors over blackface.

"You get in trouble if you are a White person who puts on blackface for Halloween or a Black person who puts on whiteface for Halloween, like … when I was a kid that was okay as long as you were dressing up as a character." Last year, talk show host Megyn Kelly defended blackface on the air. Though Kelly was already struggling with poor ratings, the episode and the resulting fury led to her ouster.

"Breaking news about another high-ranking state-wide official who finds himself embroiled in a blackface photo controversy." Now here the country is again, talking about blackface, about minstrel shows, about Jim Crow.

based on: https://www.washingtonpost.com/history/2019/02/02/northams-ugly-yearbook-photo-racist-origins-blackface/

TIPP

Knowledge of American history and society is useful for you to be able to find the solutions fast. Before listening, also highlight signal words which may give you a hint as to where you can find the answers to the questions. These signal words are marked in bold below – in the tips the words and phrases they refer to are underlined.

1 "Jim Crow […] <u>stood for hate</u> […] the <u>Jim Crow laws</u>, that made racial segregation in the South legal […]" (ll. 1 f.); "<u>symbol of inequality</u>" (l. 9)
2 The signal words "reemerged" and "recent" can guide you here: "<u>Now</u> that ugly name has <u>reemerged</u> […] thanks to the <u>recent</u> political scandals […] where both the governor and attorney general have admitted to wearing blackface in their past" (ll. 3 ff.).
3 Here the signal word for "impersonation" can be "fictional character" (l. 9 f.): "He was a <u>fictional character</u> who, to <u>entertain his audiences</u>, …"
4 Here you can mention the following aspects: "[…] danced like a buffoon and spoke with an exaggerated imitation of Black slave vernacular" (ll. 10 f.); "[…] White actors who wore tattered clothing and used shoe polish to blacken their faces […]" (ll. 12 f.).
5 "[…] who <u>drew from</u> his observations of Blacks in the South to create an extremely exaggerated and stereotypical Black buffoon." (ll. 20 f.)
6 "[…] <u>as a result</u> the character of Jim Crow spread, becoming a common stage persona" (l. 23).
7 "Davis has long argued that <u>context is key when</u> judging the use of blackface" (ll. 28 f.).
8 "[…] White artists such as Al Jolson painted their faces as they performed ragtime and blues music pioneered by African Americans. Davis <u>credits Jolson with</u> spreading Black music to White audiences and advocating for Black artists" (ll. 29 ff.).
9 "[…] talk show host <u>Megyn Kelly</u> defended blackface on the air " (ll. 36 f.).

1	According to the speaker, what did the **Jim Crow laws embody**?	• hate • (legal racial) segregation / (symbol of) (racial) inequality
2	What has **recently** led to a **new** public discussion about Jim Crow?	two high-ranking officials admitted to wearing blackface in the past / scandal about White officials (in Virginia) having worn blackface
3	What was the purpose of the Jim Crow **impersonations** in the past?	to ridicule/denigrate Blacks for entertainment / to entertain (White) audiences

4	What was **typical** of the Jim Crow stage performance? (Name two aspects.)	• buffoon-like dances / • speaking with an exaggerated black accent / • actors wearing tattered clothes / • whites using black shoe polish to appear Black
5	Where did Thomas D. Rice get his **inspiration** for the Jim Crow character from?	from his observations of Blacks (in the South)
6	What was the **consequence** of Rice's performance?	popularised the Jim Crow character / made Jim Crow a common stage persona
7	According to Daryl Davies, what does the **perception** of blackface depend on?	on the context / the time / the person's intention for wearing blackface
8	Which **positive example** of the use of blackface does Daryl Davies mention?	White artists tried to advocate Black musicians and their music
9	Which incident led to TV host **Megyn Kelly** losing her job?	she defended the use of blackface

Transcript 3   The Mindful Chef

1   If you're self-employed, you're in good company. The number of people in self-employment has been rising steadily since 2001. Natalie Donovan (ND) visited *The Mindful Chef*. It's an online recipe box delivery service and it's almost five years old and it's just been named "London & South East Start-up of the Year" in the Great
5   British Entrepreneur Awards. Co-founder Giles Humphries (GH), now at the ripe old age of 33, told Natalie how it's been.

GH: Here's myself and two friends and we were working different industries, we always had ideas and throwing ideas round to each other, but basically, I think we all enjoyed our jobs, but we realised that you can, a lot easier than before, start your
10   own business. Actually, the biggest thought was "What's the worst that could happen?"

ND: Did you feel like your, the jobs that you were doing, weren't going in the direction that you wanted to go, and that was why you decided to set back, or was it more that you had a passion about cooking and recipe boxes?

15   **GH:** I think it was two-fold really. One, we'd always had a bit of a passion to start something ourselves and we'd chat about a load of ideas over the years. And two, just looking at other friends, who had taken the plunge, taken their skills they'd honed over a few years in bigger businesses and using them to grow and develop their own businesses and I thought, hm, that's interesting cause you've got a lot
20   more control over your lifestyle and your working hours. So, that's kind of what formed the initial ideas. And then we've, we've all got a real interest in health and

wellness, all of us are sportsmen and we all, actually it was kind of a personal pain point, was coming home late, working long hours in a big company and then getting home and just being a bit too tired to think or plan and shop for the right stuff, even though we knew what we should eat.

ND: And how lang did it take you to come from the idea to actually quitting your job and setting up on your own?

GH: Probably about six months. We moved pretty quickly. It was in the summer of 2014, we were on a fishing boat, just helping out a friend actually, it was in the summer holidays, we had a week back down in Devon – we all grew up in Devon together. We saw the fish they were landing, and they were bringing back in and they'd text the local villagers and they said "We've got, you know codling etc." and the villagers'd come down and get this fresh fish. And we, the three of us, were just chatting and said: "This is amazing, this is just how a food chain should be". So this, that was one kind of lightbulb moment. And then the discussions developed from there and it was, erm, I quit my job pretty quickly, I was the first to go and it was December 2014.

ND: The business is UK-wide now. Did you know that when you started that that's what you were aiming for or did you start small?

GH: Best piece of advice, I always say is, "always start small". We had a hunch that maybe city goers would be keen on the products, but we purely did that because we were driving our own little *Del Boy Trotter* van round …

ND: So, you were delivering the boxes …

GH: So, we were delivering, yeah, we were going to the warehouse at 7 am, pack them till about 5 pm and then deliver. We'd be stuck in traffic coming back through London, Myles would be on the Instagram …

ND: … hoping you were getting a good review and a like.

GH: Yeah, yeah, yeah, going on review sites, seeing if we got any reviews, posting pictures. We started small but then we really quickly realised, once you've nailed that, you got it right, you've ironed out problems – and there were plenty of them – then you can grow slightly bigger, and when we got to that level, you know, we're now doing about, just shy of half a million ingredients through our warehouse every week but at the same time you have targets to hit and you are, you're trying to grow this business focusing on reaching quite large numbers of customers now, so, you definitely have more of a life, you know, we're not doing the packing every weekend, there's a huge team who do a phenomenal job, but the challenge is in different areas.

https://www.bbc.co.uk/sounds/play/p07xl6h5 (accessed on October 5, 2020)

TIPP

1. "[…] it's just been named 'London & South East Start-up of the Year' in the Great British Entrepreneur Awards" (l. 4 f.). The name of the prize and also the word "awards" give you hints here.
2. "[…] we always had ideas and throwing ideas round to each other (l. 7 f.)" "Throwing ideas round to each other" is like "playing with ideas" and leads you to "toying with ideas". Even if you do not know those expressions, you can find the similarity here.
3. "[…] you've got a lot more control over your lifestyle and your working hours." (l. 19 f.) Don't get confused by buzzwords such as "more satisfied in their job" but listen closely to what the new job would enable them to do.
4. "[…] personal pain point, was <u>coming home late, working long hours</u> in a big company and then getting home and just being <u>a bit too tired to</u> think or plan and <u>shop</u> for the right stuff, <u>even though we knew what we should eat</u>." (l. 22 ff.). "Coming home late" is repeated in the audio, which gives you the hint that you should now listen closely.
5. "[…] fish […] they were bringing back in and <u>they'd text the local villagers</u>" (l. 31 f.). The signal word "fish" should make you listen closely here: the expression "text the local villagers" indicates that the fishermen use modern media.
6. "[…] we were going to the warehouse at 7 am, <u>pack</u> them till about 5 pm and then deliver" (l. 44 f.). Listen closely – the word "pack" will give you a hint regarding the correct solution. Don't be distracted by buzzwords such as "traffic".
7. "[…] going on review sites, seeing if we got any reviews, <u>posting pictures</u>" (l. 48 f.). The phrase "posting pictures" indicates the correct solution. The mentioning of "Instagram" (l. 46) and getting reviews and likes (l. 47) also points towards social media rather than other forms of advertising.
8. "We started small but then we really quickly realised, once <u>you've nailed that</u>, you <u>got it right</u>, you've <u>ironed out problems</u> – and there were plenty of them – then you can grow slightly bigger […]" (l. 49 ff.).
The repetition of phrases that are used in the context of "tackling something" should be of help here.

1. *The Mindful Chef* is an online recipe box delivery service that has …
   c ✓ received a prestigious prize.

2. When the partners started their business, they …
   c ✓ had been toying with the idea for a while.

3. According to Giles Humphries, this new start would allow them to …
   d ✓ use their working time more flexibly.

4 Looking back, Humphries says that coming home late from work they …
   c ✓ were too exhausted to go shopping.

5 In the summer of 2014, Humphries observed Devon fishermen …
   d ✓ using modern media to sell their fish.

6 At the beginning of their business, Humphries and his co-founders …
   a ✓ did the packaging themselves.

7 In their marketing strategy, they relied on …
   b ✓ pictures shown on social media.

8 Success came after Humphries and his co-founders …
   d ✓ tackled initial problems successfully.

Baden-Württemberg ▪ Abiturprüfung 2022
Berufliches Gymnasium ▪ Englisch

TEIL I: LISTENING COMPREHENSION 10 VP

You will hear each recording twice. After each listening, you will have time to complete your answers.

Task 1: Book reviews 5 BE

You will hear the beginnings of five book reviews. Choose from the list (A–G) which description best applies to which book review (1–5). For each book review there is only one correct answer. There are two more descriptions than you need.

	Descriptions
A	Dealing with characters' secrets
B	Describing a character's dreams
C	Tracing a character's self-exploration
D	Inspired by very different historical events
E	Presenting the lives of prominent individuals
F	Telling the story of formerly overlooked people
G	Based on historical events and connected to current issues

Book review	1	2	3	4	5
Description					

Now listen to the recording again.

Task 2: Baroness Trumpington 14 BE

You will hear a radio report about Lady Jean Trumpington (born Jean Campbell-Harris, 1922–2018, a British politician). While listening, fill in the missing information. You need not write complete sentences. Unless otherwise specified, name one aspect.

1	Why did Lady Trumpington's departure from politics attract so much attention?	
2	Why does the host of a TV show mention the invention of television?	
3	Which incident made Lady Trumpington widely known?	
4	What is said about her education?	
5	In which two different fields of work was she active during World War II?	• •
6	Why did she return to Great Britain?	
7	What did she change in her life during her time in Cambridge?	
8	Why did she choose the title "Baroness Trumpington"?	
9	What was special about her holding her governmental position at the end of the 1980s?	
10	What did she do in Downing Street that helped her keep her position?	
11	What was her duty as Baroness in Waiting?	

12 Which interest will she continue to pursue after retiring?

Now think of the text as a whole. Tick (✓) the correct answer (a, b or c). There is only one correct answer.

13 In the radio report, Lady Trumpington's personality is presented as being

a ☐ charitable and caring.

b ☐ cautious and level-headed.

c ☐ self-confident and unconventional.

Now listen to the recording again.

| **Task 3: Sea otters** | 6 BE |

You will hear a radio report about research on sea otters in Canada. While listening, tick (✓) the correct answer (a, b or c). There is only one correct answer.
You now have two minutes to read the assignment.

1. The research focuses on the
   a ☐ effects of sea otter populations on the local economy.
   b ☐ behavioural patterns of sea otters living close to humans.
   c ☐ consequences of climate change for sea otter populations.

2. There was more seafood in the area after the Europeans had arrived because
   a ☐ sea otters were exterminated.
   b ☐ Europeans relied mainly on farming.
   c ☐ the native population was moved inland.

3. The scientists have chosen Vancouver Island for their research project because
   a ☐ university facilities are readily available.
   b ☐ a particular species of sea otters lives there.
   c ☐ the place is suitable for comparative field studies.

4. The sea otters affect the ecosystem because
   a ☐ they tend to destroy habitats of other species.
   b ☐ their feeding behaviour fosters the growth of fish.
   c ☐ they help to reduce the impact of invasive species.

5. Ecologist Edward Gregr addresses the issue that
   a ☐ visits to the area need to be regulated.
   b ☐ not everyone in the area profits in the same way.
   c ☐ too many sea otters threaten the fragile ecosystem.

6. Native Canadians living in isolated communities perceive the growing population of sea otters as
   a ☐ a potential threat.
   b ☐ a minor nuisance.
   c ☐ a welcome source of income.

Now listen to the recording again.

Lösungen

TEIL I: LISTENING COMPREHENSION

Transcript 1   Book reviews

Snippet/book 1: Welcome to Book Club and a novel that's set in the aftermath of the First World War but crackles with contemporary relevance. James Meek's novel *The People's Act of Love* is set in the wastes of Siberia in 1919. And in a way, it is a Russian novel, because its action springs from the turmoil of that country in its dark history.

Snippet/book 2: Hello and welcome to Book Club from Swansea. Sheers's book is a psychological thriller that mixes suspense – Michael, the central character, tries to conceal an awful event out of fear – with a story of the relationship between two men who both have something to hide.

Snippet/book 3: If you look at *The New York Times* for October 4th, 1951, you will see two headlines jostling together on the front page, one reporting that "Giants win over the Brooklyn Dodgers in a famous baseball game", the other saying, "Soviets explode atomic bomb". Well, when Don DeLillo looked at those headlines in the early nineties, 40 years on, the prickle of excitement started him on a journey of the imagination that led to *Underworld*.

Snippet/book 4: Hello and welcome to Book Club and a biographical feast. We're talking this month about the story of two interlocked families, and at the head of them, the two most glamorous figures of the late Victorian stage, Sir Henry Irving and Ellen Terry. They're the joint subjects of one of our most admired literary biographers, Michael Holroyd, now in his eighties, who's our guest today.

Snippet/book 5: Hello and welcome to Book Club. This month's book is funny and breezy, but don't be misled by that. *Rachel's Holiday* is also a journey into darkness with Rachel discovering the depths of her drug addiction and its threat to her whole life. Her holiday is, in fact, a trip into rehab, away from the high life she's been enjoying in New York to a clinic in Dublin, the Cloisters, where she imagines that she'll get away from it all, but instead discovers more about herself than she expected.

based on: bbc.co.uk/sounds/play/m000dxtp; bbc.co.uk/sounds/play/m0007b4t; bbc.co.uk/sounds/play/b07sxttn; bbc.co.uk/sounds/play/b072htqw; bbc.co.uk/sounds/play/m000fw1j

> **TIPP**

You do not have a lot of time to read through the task, so concentrate on highlighting the keywords which sum up the main idea of a description. Also mark words you think are essential for comprehension. You will have a very short break before and in between sets to look them up, but do not overestimate the time frame. The listening comprehension in your exam takes its complexity not only from the level of sophistication of the audio files, but also from the speed with which you have to solve the tasks.

- **1 – G:** The key phrases in the description are "historical events" as well as "connected to current issues" (= "contemporary relevance, l. 2), which is the main difference when compared to description D, which only speaks of "historical events". It also differs from D in that it does not deal with "very different historical events" but rather focuses on a specific historical period of a specific country.
- **2 – A:** The key word here is "secret", which is indirectly mentioned several times: The review talks about the protagonist "[trying] to conceal" (ll. 6 f.) something and about two men "[having] something to hide" (l. 8).
- **3 – D:** The fact that the review talks about "headlines jostling" (l. 10) points towards "very different historical events", as mentioned in D. If you don't know the word "jostling", the headlines give you an even stronger clue: One is about a baseball game (ll. 10 f.), the other about the explosion of an atomic bomb (ll. 11 f.), which do not have anything in common.
- **4 – E:** Finding the correct solution can be tricky here, because you might mistake the word "interlocked" (l. 16) for "overlooked". In this case, you might be tempted to choose F ("story of overlooked people") as an answer. It is, however, stated that the book deals with "the two most glamorous figures of the late Victorian stage" (l. 17) which then leaves E ("prominent individuals") as the correct solution.
- **5 – C:** This review hints at the correct description quite often. It is about "self-exploration", which is expressed in phrases like "journey into darkness" (l. 21), with the protagonist "discovering the depths of her drug addiction" (l. 22) and "[discovering] more about herself than she expected" (l. 25).

Book review	1	2	3	4	5
Description	G	A	D	E	C

| **Transcript 2** | Baroness Trumpington |

Edward Stourton: It should surely not come as a shock when a nonagenarian decides to retire. But Lady Trumpington's decision to leave the House of Lords when she reaches 95 this month made a splash. Perhaps that's because she's been part of the place for so long. No one can quite imagine the scene without her.

TV host: It would be ungallant of me to tell you Her Ladyship's age. So let's just say she was born before this programme started. And before BBC One started. And before television started. Please welcome Baroness Trumpington.

Stourton: She began among pearls and ermine, and she's ending her long career in similar territory. On the way, she's lived our history and known most of the people who made it. But she only really became famous in her late eighties when she was caught by the cameras making a V-sign at one of her fellow peers, as the comedian Jack Whitehall reminded her on "Have I Got News for You?".

Jack Whitehall: Did you regret swearing at him or …?

Baroness Trumpington: No, because I regretted what he said, which was that people of my age were starting to look very, very, very old. Well, wouldn't you do that if you …?

Jack Whitehall: Yeah, I can see …

Stourton: Jean Campbell-Harris was born in 1922. Her father was a former major in the Bengal Lancers with the right connections. Her mother was the heir to a Chicago paint fortune. Her formal education was limited, as was often the way for women then. And she says she's never taken an exam. But finishing school in Paris gave her good French and German. The war began when she was 16.

Old news report: Down on the farm, the land girls are doing their bit and a bit more.

Stourton: Like thousands of other young women, Jean Campbell-Harris was sent to work as a land girl, filling the gap left when the countryside's young men went to fight. In 1940, she took her language skills to the secret codebreaking centre of Bletchley Park. She was a cipher clerk. Jean worked on Madison Avenue in the post-war Mad Men days, and it was in the United States that she met her very English husband, Alan Barker, a historian, then working at the Ivy League University, Yale. His career brought him back to a teaching post at Eton and then to the headmaster's job at the Leys, a private school in Cambridge. *[excerpt from song]* And it was during her years as a headmaster's wife that Jean Barker, as she then was, really turned her attention to politics.

Georgina Morley: She became a councillor in Cambridge and then ultimately mayor of Cambridge, and I think she rather loved being mayor.

Stourton: Local politics was a long way from life in Mayfair and Manhattan, and her early political career was hard graft. She tried and failed to become an MP. The political scene was dominated by another powerful woman, Margaret Thatcher. In 1980, Jean Barker was given a peerage by the new Tory government. She already had contacts in the House of Lords, including the Tory peer, Viscount Astor, whose mother had been Jean's friend and fellow clerk at Bletchley.

Viscount Astor: Jean took to the House of Lords like a duck to water, as it were, because she could actually kind of deflate someone who was being pompous, for example.

Stourton: There remained the little matter of deciding on a title. Her reputation for a robust speaking style was already established, so she rejected Baroness Barker. She explained her final decision to the prominent eighties Tory John Gummer, now Lord Deben.

Lord Deben: So, she said I had to choose the village nearest to me. And there were two possibilities. One was Trumpington and the other was Six Mile Bottom. She thought that was not a good idea. So, Trumpington it was.

Stourton: Lady Trumpington's husband Alan died after a stroke in 1988, leaving her a widow in her mid-sixties. She was serving as a minister of Agriculture at the time, the first ever woman minister there, and threw herself into her work. She survived at the ministry when John Major succeeded Margaret Thatcher until …

Georgina Morley: At one point she was called into Downing Street. And John Major, it turned out, had decided that the time had come for her to retire from the front bench, and she was not expecting this. And she told me afterwards, shamelessly, that she cried. Whereupon the Prime Minister patted her on the shoulder and said, "There, there, all right then, well, never mind, we'll leave you as you are." So, she stayed on.

Stourton: By 1992, she was the oldest ever serving woman minister, and during John Major's second term, she became a Baroness in Waiting, representing the Queen on formal occasions until the Tories lost power in 1997. Lady Trumpington isn't giving up all her passions. Her enthusiasm for horse racing, for example, is as fierce as ever. But her son, Adam, says that by giving up the Lords, she's giving up more than a job.

Adam Barker: The Lords became her family.

based on: bbc.co.uk/sounds/play/b098bqr1

> **TIPP**
>
> This task requires an in-depth knowledge of vocabulary, the ability to distinguish between several native speakers talking, and the skill to understand various accents of British English. You also have to cope with inferior sound quality in bits of historic audio documents. However, do not worry too much, as you can rely on the order of the questions following the chronology of the recording and you mostly need to note down only one aspect out of several mentioned.
>
> **1** There are several reasons why Lady Trumpington's decision to "leave the House of Lords" (l. 2) or, in other words "politics", attracted attention or "made a splash" (l. 3): "she's been part of the place for so long" (ll. 3 f.), "No one can quite imagine the scene without her." (l. 4), and also "she reaches 95 this month" (ll. 2 f.)

2. By mentioning the invention of television the host reveals Lady Trumpington's age in an indirect and humorous way ("It would be ungallant of me to tell you Her Ladyship's age." l. 5): "So let's just say <u>she was born</u> before this programme started. And before BBC One started. And <u>before television</u> <u>started</u>." (ll. 5 ff.)

3. You do not need to know that the "V-sign" is a rude gesture (when the palm is facing towards the person making the sign) – it is enough to recognize the host mentioning that "she only really became famous in her late eighties when she was caught by the cameras making a V-sign at one of her fellow peers" (ll. 10 f.). In the next sentence it becomes clear that she was swearing at him (l. 13).

4. The show continues with milestones in Baroness Trumpington's life. Be careful, however, because this task only asks for <u>Trumpington's education</u>. You only need to note down one aspect from lines 20–22: "[…] formal education was limited […] she's never taken an exam […] finishing school in Paris […] good French and German."

5. Listen closely here: The short clipping from a wartime news report serves as a distractor and the term "land girl(s)" (ll. 23 ff.) is mentioned quite fast, meaning that she worked on a farm during the war. Her second job as a "cipher clerk" (l. 27) is not only hard to understand, but also no longer common and you need to know "clerk" as another word for "secretary" or "office worker". Bletchley Park was a facility of the British Intelligence Service to decode secret German messages in World War II. If you know that, you can also give "intelligence work" or "code breaking" as an answer.

6. Here, you need to deduct the answer from what was said about Trumpington's husband, whom she met in the United States (ll. 28 f.) and who was "a historian, then working at […] Yale. His career brought him back to […] Eton and then to […] a private school in Cambridge." (l. 29 ff.), so Jean Barker, as she was now called, became "a headmaster's wife" (l. 32) in England.

7. In order to answer this question correctly, you must not lose track of the audio. It ends with the story of Trumpington's husband who got a job in Cambridge. And here, the Baroness "turned her attention to politics" (l. 33) by becoming councillor and mayor (ll. 34 f.) there.

8. Listen particularly closely after the keyword "title" (l. 44). As Trumpington "rejected [the title of] Baroness Barker" (l. 45), she then had "to choose the village nearest to [her]" (l. 48) and as she refused being called "Six Mile Bottom", she chose the other village called "Trumpington" (ll. 49 f.).

9. Pay attention when the year 1988 is mentioned (l. 51), which points towards the question of "her governmental position at the end of the 1980s". The audio says that "she was serving as a minister of Agriculture at the time, the first ever woman minister there […]" (l. 52 f.) and that she still was "at the ministry when John Major succeeded Margaret Thatcher" (ll. 43 f.).

10 Here, "Downing Street" is the key word. Pay attention to what Lady Trumpington did when she was asked to resign by John Major, then Prime Minister: "[…] she cried" (ll. 57 f.), which lead to "[…] the Prime Minister [patting] her on the shoulder" and leaving her in office (ll. 58 ff.).
11 The moment the audio mentions "Baroness in Waiting" (l. 62), it is explained that she was "representing the Queen on formal occasions" (ll. 62 f.).
12 This information is also given very fast and rather at the end of the audio when your concentration might be decreasing. It is stated that the Baroness has a passion for horse racing (l. 64), so you can deduce that this is what she will continue to follow after retiring.
13 Here you need to understand the general character of Baroness Trumpington. By having a look at your answers in 1–12, there is nothing that hints towards "charitable and caring". If that were the case, the audio would have given some examples. The same goes for "cautious and level-headed". A person who became a politician without formal education, went to the United States on her own, gave inappropriate hand signs towards a colleague, and was still active in her 90s can be nothing more than "self-confident and unconventional".

1	Why did Lady Trumpington's departure from politics attract so much attention?	She was part of the "House of Lords" for so long. / No one can imagine the House of Lords / politics without her. / She was already 95 when she retired.
2	Why does the host of a TV show mention the invention of television?	to indirectly tell the audience Lady Trumpington's (advanced) age / because Lady Trumpington had been born before TV was invented (and thereby alluding to her advanced age) / to introduce Lady Trumpington in a humorous way
3	Which incident made Lady Trumpington widely known?	making the V-sign / making a rude gesture / swearing (at a fellow peer)
4	What is said about her education?	*one of the following:* • limited formal education (typical for women at that time) / • has never taken an exam / • finished school in Paris / • good at French and German
5	In which two different fields of work was she active during World War II?	*two of the following:* • farm work / (work as a) land girl • (work as a) cipher clerk / code breaking / intelligence work / office work
6	Why did she return to Great Britain?	(She returned) because of her husband's job. / She followed her husband.

7	What did she change in her life during her time in Cambridge?	started her political career / turned her attention to politics / became councillor / mayor
8	Why did she choose the title "Baroness Trumpington"?	She did not like the other options. / She chose the name of a village closest to her home.
9	What was special about her holding her governmental position at the end of the 1980s?	first female Minister of Agriculture / first woman holding that position in Great Britain / stayed in office when the Prime Minister changed
10	What did she do in Downing Street that helped her keep her position?	She cried. / She made the Prime Minister feel sorry for her.
11	What was her duty as Baroness in Waiting?	representing the Queen on formal occasions
12	Which interest will she continue to pursue after retiring?	horse racing

13 In the radio report, Lady Trumpington's personality is presented as being

c ☑ self-confident and unconventional.

Transcript 3 Sea otters

Ari Shapiro *(host)*: Let's talk about sea otters. They float on the water, cuddle their little babies. Same time, they're voracious eaters that gobble up shellfish. And that has brought them into conflict with people who rely on shellfish for their livelihoods. NPR's Nell Greenfield-Boyce reports that scientists have now assessed the economic impact of restoring sea otters to their historic homes.

Nell Greenfield-Boyce *(byline)*: Sea otters are pretty big. They can weigh 60 pounds or more. To survive in the cold waters of the Northern Pacific, they need to eat a lot.

Jane Watson: And so a sea otter is going to eat about a quarter of its body mass, its body weight, in food each day.

Greenfield-Boyce: Jane Watson is a researcher with Vancouver Island University in Canada. She says historically sea otters coexisted with Indigenous people. But when the Europeans arrived, hunters with the fur trade wiped the otters out.

Watson: All of a sudden, all of the prey that otters eat no longer had their principal predator eating them anymore.

Greenfield-Boyce: Clams, crabs, sea urchins – their populations took off, and people got used to the abundance. Well, a few decades ago, sea otters were reintroduced to the west coast of Vancouver Island. Edward Gregr is an ecologist at the University of

British Columbia. He says further down the coast from where the otters now live, there's another spot where the otters haven't yet moved in.

20 **Edward Gregr:** And so we thought, this is, you know, this is a perfect natural experiment to compare what the ecosystem looks like with and without sea otters.

Greenfield-Boyce: In the journal *Science*, they say otters do eat up clams and crabs worth millions of dollars. They also devour sea urchins, and that allows kelp to flourish. The kelp supports fish species that are worth a lot of money. What's more,
25 tourists will pay to watch the otters frolic. Gregr says, all in all, the financial benefits of otters are more than seven times greater than the losses. But, he says ...

Gregr: We want to make sure we don't lose sight of the caveats around that, mainly the fact that, you know, these costs and benefits are not going to be distributed equally across fisheries or communities.

30 **Greenfield-Boyce:** Tourism, for example, isn't necessarily a realistic or attractive option for people who live in remote areas where access to food is a real issue. Barbara Wilson is a member of the Haida Nation who's studied Indigenous people's feelings about the sea otters.

Barbara Wilson: The impact for us is fairly critical.

35 **Greenfield-Boyce:** She says Canadian law currently protects the otters. The otters have a right to eat, but so do people. Nell Greenfield-Boyce, NPR News.

© 2020 National Public Radio, Inc. News report titled "What Happens When Sea Otters Eat 15 Pounds of Shellfish A Day" was originally broadcast on NPR's All Things Considered on June 11, 2020, and is used with the permission of NPR. Any unauthorized duplication is strictly prohibited.

TIPP

This task can be difficult insofar as the vocabulary is rather sophisticated or technical and the correct answer is often hidden behind complex expressions. Take your time before the first listening round to look up keywords to which you should pay attention while listening to the text.

1 The scientists are doing research on the impact sea otters have on the local economy: in lines 2 f. the host mentions "[gobbling up] shellfish [...] brought [the otters] into conflict with people who rely on shellfish for their livelihoods" and in lines 4 f. he says that "scientists have now assessed the economic impact of restoring sea otters to their historic homes".

2 The audio mentions that otters were "wiped out" (another word for being "exterminated") by the Europeans (l. 12). Next, the podcast explains that "all of the prey that otters eat no longer had their principal predator eating them anymore" (ll. 13 f.), which eventually led to an "abundance" (ll. 15 f.) of seafood in the area".

3. A scientist explains why <u>Vancouver Island is the perfect place for a "natural experiment to compare</u> what the ecosystem looks like with and without sea otters." (ll. 20 f.). A key word is "comparative", which is the adjective of the verb "compare" that is mentioned in the audio.
4. Here you need to find out that in places where there are sea otters the fish population increases. The following sentence explains why: "[The <u>otters</u>] also <u>devour sea urchins</u>, and <u>that allows kelp to flourish. The kelp supports fish species</u> that are worth a lot of money." (l. 23 f.), which means that "their feeding behaviour fosters the growth of fish". The other options ("destroying habitats" and "help to reduce the impact of invasive species") are not mentioned in the text.
5. The solution can be found in lines 28 f.: "[…] these costs and <u>benefits are not going to be distributed equally</u> across fisheries or communities." A potential threat to the ecosystem is not mentioned in the audio and although one might be tempted to tick a) because of tourists visiting the area (l. 30), this is not called an issue at all.
6. The correct solution lies in the quote by Barbara Wilson, who is a representative of the Haida and expresses "Indigenous people's feelings about the sea otters" (ll. 32 f.). She explicitly states that "The impact [of the growing population of sea otters] for us is fairly critical." (l. 34). This is too severe a way of talking about that issue to call it "a minor nuisance", while "a welcome source of income" is not mentioned at all.

1 The research focusses on the
   a ✓ effects of sea otter populations on the local economy.

2 There was more seafood in the area after the Europeans had arrived because
   a ✓ sea otters were exterminated.

3 The scientists have chosen Vancouver Island for their research project because
   c ✓ the place is suitable for comparative field studies.

4 The sea otters affect the ecosystem because
   b ✓ their feeding behaviour fosters the growth of fish.

5 Ecologist Edward Gregr addresses the issue that
   b ✓ not everyone in the area profits in the same way.

6 Native Canadians living in isolated communities perceive the growing population of sea otters as
   a ✓ a potential threat.

Baden-Württemberg ▪ Abiturprüfung 2023
Berufliches Gymnasium ▪ Englisch

Um Ihnen die Prüfung 2023 schnellstmöglich zur Verfügung stellen zu können, bringen wir sie in digitaler Form heraus.

Sobald die Original-Prüfungsaufgaben 2023 freigegeben sind, können sie als PDF auf der Plattform **MyStark** heruntergeladen werden (Zugangscode vgl. Umschlaginnenseite vorne im Buch).

Aktuelle Prüfung

www.stark-verlag.de/mystark